LIVE
TO
MAKE
MEN
FREE

LIVE TO MAKE MEN FREE

AN AMERICAN'S ODYSSEY IN THE WORLD'S FIRST ATHEIST NATION

ROGER SHERRARD WITH ART MOORE

RESOLUTE PRESS

CONTENTS

DISCLAIMER

This work depicts actual events in the life of Roger Sherrard as truthfully as recollection permits. All persons named are actual individuals. The views and opinions expressed belong to the author and do not necessarily reflect the views and opinions of Advocates International. These events began more than three decades ago and do not represent the ongoing work of Advocates International. The current Advocates International organization and its board members have not participated in the writing and publication of this book.

PROLOGUE

ON MARCH 24, 1992, I received two faxes at the law office of Sherrard, McGonagle, Green and Johnson on Front Street in Poulsbo, Washington. The letters, arriving almost simultaneously, were from people who didn't know each other. One came from some twenty-five hundred miles to the southwest in Hawaii. The other from more than five thousand miles to the east, in Vienna, Austria.

But the messages were the same. An isolated nation tucked in the southeast corner of Europe had broken free of five decades of Stalinist rule. Albania—the only country to have completely banned religion—was looking for "a new identity and a new national purpose," as one fax put it.

A broken but resilient people, they were sorting out how to govern themselves for the first time in perhaps six centuries. Leaders of the newly formed Ministry of Justice, along with other political leaders, lawyers, civil servants, and law students, were eager for help, I was told.

And they sought assistance from, of all nations, the number one sworn enemy of the old regime, the United States of America.

Unlike the Soviet Eastern bloc, Albania's communist regime had banned American citizens from crossing its borders. But as early as the winter of 1990-91, Americans were among the first to bring humanitarian relief.

One fax on that March day came from Mark Spengler, the vice-chancellor of University of the Nations in Hilo, Hawaii. He said his colleagues had met Ministry of Justice officials who were asking for seminars, mentoring relationships, and other kinds of "retraining" to help establish "law and justice under democracy."

The other fax came from Art Moore, the co-author of this book, who already had connected me with a law school in Sofia, Bulgaria, that sought similar help from the West.

On my initial trip to Bulgaria in 1991, I was joined by Sam Ericsson, who had just stepped down as the director of the Christian Legal Society. As we waited for our flights home at the Sofia airport, Sam and I contemplated where all we had experienced might lead. We were drawn to the biblical story of Esther. We adopted chapter 4, verse 13 as the theme for this extraordinary assignment: "And who knows but that you have come to royal position for such a time as this?"

Spengler, whom I had never met, opened his faxed letter to me recalling that the book of Esther tells the story of an unlikely figure "God had prepared to perform a strategic role in the furtherance of his plans for the Jewish people." He concluded his opening paragraph with the words "for such a time as this."

On one hand, I was just an estate-tax lawyer from Poulsbo, a Norwegian-immigrant village across the Puget Sound from Seattle. At first glance, there seemed to be no earthly reason why I should have been the recipient of a call to help a devastated nation establish a "new order."

But in retrospect, in ways I never could have planned, I had been prepared for this moment. For one, through an improbable sequence of events, I had been thrust into a seminal case in the Washington state Supreme Court that became my first training in constitutional law.

I was a graduate of West Point, but I never should have been admitted. (I'll tell you why later). After graduation in 1966, I completed Airborne and Ranger school and was deployed in the Cold War-era fight against communism. Despite my inexperience—the Army was severely under-staffed at this early stage of the Vietnam War—I was assigned as an armor platoon leader and company commander on the Cold War's Eastern front in Germany. In 1968, I was hired as aide de camp by Maj. Gen. John S. Hughes, who, a few months later, became commander over all the troops in Southern Europe. We moved with him to his new assignment in Vicenza, Italy. I eventually was deployed to Vietnam in the fall of 1969, where, as an infantry company commander, I led men in combat.

It turned out, after all, as I later was told, that the Albanians had sought an American lawyer who knew something about constitutional law and had never worked for a large corporation or the government.

But you couldn't have found that person at a more obscure law office in America.

On the first of more than fifty visits to Albania spanning more than twenty-five years, I remember the uncanny feeling of entering another world. At Rinas International Airport in Tirana, a donkey-drawn cart ferried our bags to the terminal. Upon setting foot in the dirt parking lot, I was immediately swarmed like a rock star by boys with smudged faces pleading for gum as chickens scampered among them. On the eleven-mile, bone-jarring drive to the capital city, we slowed for wobbly, horse-drawn carts manned by grim, wizened figures. Typically during that time, drivers would come to a full stop behind a Mao-era Chinese truck as the driver tried to re-engage the ignition with a hand crank inserted through the grill.

As I came to know and love Albanian presidents, prime ministers, chief justices, lawyers, teachers, drivers, bodyguards, and street sweepers, it became clear that severe political oppression and economic poverty had not made this irrepressible, lavishly hospitable people impoverished in spirit.

These image-bearers of their creator had been victims of ideas, which, as my mother never ceased to remind me, have consequences.

A truly ancient people, some scholars trace them to the Illyrians, who lived in the region when it was known as Illyricum. The apostle Paul, according to local lore, walked the street still known as the Via Egnatia in the central Albanian city of Elbasan. The book of Romans confirms he traveled "from Jerusalem all the way around to Illyricum."

After nearly five hundred years of Ottoman Turkish rule, a brief police-state monarchy, and five decades of Stalinism, the consequences of ideas were evident to the long-suffering Albanian people.

On my first trip to the Balkan nation, I sat around a table in an executive boardroom with government leaders. In an informal discussion, I was invited to explain some of the universal principles of liberty embraced by America's Founders.

At the heart of the Declaration of Independence, I said, is the belief that our rights as human beings are granted to us not by a government, but by our creator. Any rights granted by a government can be removed by a government. The purpose of government is only to recognize and protect the unalienable rights that already exist.

Built upon that foundation is the separation of powers, without which America as a republic could not function. Under Enver Hoxha's communist regime in Albania, my new friends explained to me, there was no separation between the executive and the judiciary. The dictator rendered the final verdict in legal cases in which he had an interest.

Among the Albanian leaders who began to embrace concepts despised by the old regime was a University of Tirana law professor and parliament member named Zef Brozi.

My focus on Zef's story in the first chapter is not to set him apart from the many Albanians my wife, Katoo, and I count as dear friends. My intent, before telling the story chronologically, is to give you a glimpse of what is truly at stake.

Even in the new Albania, as he rose to the position of chief justice of the Supreme Court, Zef's courageous practice and defense of the principles of liberty and the necessity of an independent judiciary to establish a just society had consequences.

1

IN WITH THE OLD

AT 5 A.M. ON SATURDAY, NOVEMBER 4, 1995, Zef Brozi was jolted awake by a knock on the front door of his apartment in Albania's capital, Tirana.

Only seven weeks earlier, the Albanian Parliament, under "orders" from President Sali Berisha, had removed Zef as chief justice of the Supreme Court. The once isolated Balkan nation—by far, Europe's poorest—was four years into a chaotic post-communist era in which the old totalitarian sensibilities were welcomed by some as respites of order and civil peace.

Eastern Europe's most brutal regime—under which nearly every family suffered the horror of a member punished for "crimes against the state"—had collapsed after half a century of rule. Amid the chaos that followed, Berisha became the nation's first freely elected head of state and the first non-communist leader in fifty-three years.

A professed champion of liberal democracy, the former cardiologist of dictator Enver Hoxha had been welcomed to the Oval Office by President George H.W. Bush as a man with whom Washington could work.

But when newspapers criticized Berisha and his Democratic Party of Albania, the president ordered that the presses be shut down. And when Zef's court ruled contrary to Berisha's wishes in two cases against journalists who were sentenced to prison, the president summoned the chief justice to his office.

"Why didn't you talk to me before you made that decision?" he asked Zef, according to Zef's account.

The chief justice pulled the keys to his judicial chamber from his pocket and tossed them on the president's desk.

"Mr. President," he said, pausing. "If you want to be both president and chief justice, here you go."

Zef kept the keys and his job, but on September 21, 1995, the Parliament, without constitutional cause, voted to remove him from office.

Berisha, however, was not done with Zef. Fearing he might have created an opposition leader, the president sent dozens of law enforcement officers and members of his secret police to surround the apartment of Zef and Diana Brozi.

In the predawn darkness of that November Saturday, a voice at the door demanded entrance.

"We want your passport. Hand over your passport."

Zef, able to see outside through a camera installed by his nephew, recognized members of "Berisha's gang." And the chief justice had plenty of evidence to surmise that their intent was "to take me away and make me disappear."

He asked the officers at the door if they had any authorization from the court or a prosecutor.

They had none. Zef refused to open the door, and he called the US Embassy, which had promised to dispatch help in case of the kind of trouble he now faced.

'IF YOU HAVE AN ESCAPE PLAN, IMPLEMENT IT NOW'

Later that Saturday, bolstered now by the witness of US officials and journalists, Zef handed over his diplomatic passport.

The Brozis' apartment remained under the watch of the secret police. But stripped of his passport, Zef was no longer seen as a flight risk.

Meanwhile, I received word from a White House official that house arrest was the least of Zef's problems.

"I will deny ever telling you this, but we have evidence that your friend is going to die in a car accident," the official informed me. "If you have an escape plan, implement it now."

What Berisha didn't know is that Zef had applied for a personal passport the day after his removal from office. The escape plan we had devised with the US Embassy went like this: Zef would call the embassy and say, "This is Zef Brozi, I want to speak to Carlo." Carlo was Carl Siebentritt, the political officer at the embassy. Before the call was even forwarded to Siebentritt, a car would be dispatched to Zef's apartment carrying an embassy representative, his passport, and plane tickets.

In the predawn hours of Sunday, November 12, 1995, Zef and Diana slipped through the now relaxed watch of "Berisha's gang" to a car. Escorted by an embassy official, they were on their way to Rinas International Airport, which then amounted to a small building adjacent to a crumbling tarmac surrounded by fields of cattle just outside the capital city.

Zef and Diana breathed deeply as they settled into their seats and the door closed on a Soviet-era Tupolev jetliner bound for Budapest that would connect them with a flight to New York.

Cleared for takeoff, the Malev Hungarian Airlines jet bounced down the pockmarked runway. Suddenly, the high-pitched whine of the engines began to recede, and the plane came to a stop.

After some fifteen interminable minutes, the jetliner began to taxi, and soon, the Brozis were separated from their homeland.

'YOU ARE VERY LUCKY, VERY BLESSED TO BE ALIVE'

Two days after arriving in New York City, a call came for Zef from a man with an English accent who didn't immediately identify himself. Jarringly, he was familiar with details of Zef's dramatic exit from Albania.

"Did the plane stop after it began to taxi?" the man asked.

"Yes," Zef replied.

"Then it stopped after it almost took off?"

"Yes."

"Do you know why?"

"Mechanical problems?" Zef offered.

The Englishman, who Zef later learned had been an adviser to Berisha, explained that the president and the secret police thought they had prevented Zef from leaving the country by taking his diplomatic passport.

Orders had been given to stop the plane and remove Zef and his wife. And then, mysteriously, the orders were rescinded.

"I think the man at the US Embassy and others monitoring my situation called Washington," Zef later said.

"I didn't ask, because some things were not for me to know—how they did it."

Zef recalled that he had been regularly followed by secret police during the two years prior to his abrupt departure.

"Friends told me they had information about two situations. They said, 'You are very lucky, very blessed, to be alive.' They knew more than I know even now."

'THE JUDGES ARE TOO STRONG'

Zef grew up under Hoxha's tyranny in the northern district of Mirdita. "Mirdita" is the greeting for "good day" in Albanian. He was among the first Albanian jurists of the nation's new era to embrace the alien concept of the separation of powers and an independent judiciary bound by the rule of law.

From the moment I arrived in Albania for the first time in 1992 to this day, my intent has been chiefly to come alongside Albanian leaders, at their request, and offer principles and guidelines. It was up to them to decide what was right for Albania.

America is far from a perfect nation, I frequently reminded my Albanian friends, and they could learn from our failures as well as our successes.

Through helping them write a new constitution, judicial conferences, seminars, mentorship, and giving resources of various kinds—but mostly through enduring personal relationships—we've tried to communicate principles that have made America an exceptional nation in world history.

But principles possess no power unless they take root in people of character such as Zef. There would be other significant friendships to come, with other Albanian chief justices, and with presidents and prime ministers as well as scores of judges and lawyers. But Zef grew close enough to ask me to be the co-best man at his wedding.

And even at the celebration of his marriage, there were signs of trouble ahead. The service was held in July 1995 at the Catholic cathedral on Kavajë Street in Tirana, which during the communist era was seized by the atheist government and turned into a movie theater.

At the reception, I found myself in an uncomfortable conversation with a ranking member of parliament.

"The judges are too strong," he said. "We've got to rein them in."

"What does that mean?" I asked.

"Well, we haven't decided how we're going to do it, but we've got to show that the executive is in control."

A QUESTION FOR THE US SUPREME COURT JUSTICE

During the communist era, the chief justice was a member of the Communist Party, and Zef often explained to me how difficult it was for Albanians to grasp the idea that a chief justice could say no to the president.

One year before his dramatic escape, we brought Zef and several members of Albania's Supreme Court to the US Supreme Court in

Washington for a visit. It was December 1994, and our host was then-Associate Justice Sandra Day O'Connor.

Zef, already under intense pressure back home, saw an immediate opportunity, he later recalled, to send a message to his judicial colleagues. But at the time, we thought he had lost his mind in the presence of this esteemed member of America's highest court.

"What would you do if President Clinton asked you for a favor for a case that is to be heard in the Supreme Court?" he asked O'Connor in Albanian.

The interpreter translated for the justice.

"I don't understand the question," O'Connor replied.

Zef repeated it slowly for the translator.

O'Connor appeared perplexed, if not perturbed.

"That will never happen. The president cannot tell a justice how to decide a case," she said.

Zef pressed further. "But suppose it happens."

She replied, "Then the president would be in trouble."

But in the Albania of the early 1990s, it was a chief justice who refused to take a call from "the red phone" who drew trouble.

Born in 1958, Zef was the youngest of eleven children of uneducated farmers who, as he described it, worked hard and avoided causing trouble for themselves under the strict rule of Enver Hoxha, an ally of Mao Zedong.

Many close friends suffered as political prisoners, he said.

"But if you just worked and kept your mouth closed, you were not in that kind of danger."

SOUND OF FREEDOM

Albanians might be excused for thinking that after nearly five centuries of Ottoman Turkish rule, a brief monarchist police state, and five decades in a Stalinist dystopia, the act of opening their shades to the West for the first time would simply let in the sunshine of freedom.

I remember lying awake in bed in the middle of a beastly hot summer night at the home of a lawyer friend in Tirana. The windows were open, and although others must have desired sleep as well, boom boxes were blaring. It seemed that most of the town was outside in the streets partying.

In one sense, it was the sound of freedom I was hearing. Accustomed to self-censoring even conversations inside their homes, in this giddy, new world, everything seemed permissible.

In those early days, I had many discussions with Albanian jurists and politicians about fundamental concepts such as freedom.

What is freedom? Is it the liberty to do anything one wishes? What happens when my freedoms conflict with another citizen's freedoms?

Alexis de Tocqueville famously studied America's experiment in freedom in the 1830s, concluding that sustainable civic freedom is the freedom not to do anything one wishes, but to do what is good and right.

The French diplomat-philosopher saw for himself how a strong civil society with faith as the anchor made governance by the people possible. To the extent that citizens are guided by an internal moral compass, peace and prosperity flourish without the need for big government.

As I so often told my Albanian friends, America's commitment to its declared ideal of liberty as the freedom to do good certainly has been tested. Slavery, Jim Crow laws, and many other national sins often have come up in conversations.

My youngest son, Toby, joined me on a trip to Albania, in 2001, after his graduation from Washington State University.

On our last night, the president invited us for dinner along with two key legal figures in the Bush-Gore election lawsuits of 2000 whom I had brought to Albania to consult on election laws, Judge John Kuder and attorney Roger Magnuson.

Prior to the dinner, we were treated to a show at the Soviet-built amphitheater in Tirana, featuring the US Army glee club.

At dinner, Albania's chief justice at the time, Thimio Kondi, invited Toby to ask any question of the hosts. Along with the president, they included the speaker of parliament, the minister of justice, and several other government officials.

"I don't understand why Albanians like Americans so much," Toby said.

Thimio went first.

"We like America because you're the only country in the history of the world that gives freedom to the countries it conquers," he said.

"And not only did you give Europe freedom, you helped rebuild it so it could remain free."

Thimio noted that Albanians don't agree with everything America has done.

"But we trust you more than anybody else."

2

MANY FATHERS

I was in the third grade when my father, Jean, died, leaving my mother to raise me and my three older brothers, Jean, Don, and Jerry.

I missed my father dearly, but I never felt fatherless. My mother, Marian, intentionally brought father figures into my life. Three who stood out were Joe DeWeese, Tommy Graham, and Eddie Le Penske.

Eddie was a legendary United Airlines pilot who transported troops around the Pacific during World War II. Tommy also flew for United.

Joe, a Boeing engineer, was the enforcer. I got into a lot of trouble at Des Moines Elementary School, on the shore of Puget Sound, south of Seattle. When I became particularly unruly with my mother, she would say, "Do you want Joe to come down?"

Nothing more needed to be said or done.

When I was preparing to go into the fifth grade, my mother went to the principal.

"He has enough women in his life," she said. "He needs a male teacher for the fifth grade."

A woman typically didn't make demands like that in those days. But my mother wasn't typical.

She had taken over my father's trucking business, Skagit River Motor Lines. The potential buyers had thought they would wait a year or two, and she would run it into the ground. Then they would swoop in and take it over.

The license to carry small loads was controlled by the state. If you had a license for a particular route, you had the exclusive rights. My father had the rights for the Seattle-to-Bellingham route, serviced by about twenty trucks.

One day, a truck was behind schedule, and my mother stepped in to help load it.

She came home that night and told us the company had been shut down for a day or two by the Teamsters Union, because she wasn't a member. She understood that the order came from Dave Beck, the legendary president of the International Brotherhood of Teamsters from 1952 to 1957, who was succeeded by Jimmy Hoffa.

Beck, who grew up in Seattle, famously was grilled by future senator Robert F. Kennedy before the United States Senate Select Committee on Improper Activities in Labor and Management.

My mother wasn't afraid of Dave Beck, either.

THE LONG GRAY LINE

One of the many gifts my mother passed on to me was her tenacity. But her persistence and single-mindedness were graced with wisdom, and I've been trying to catch up to her ever since.

On the football field at Highline High School in Burien, Washington, for example, my big heart and small frame collided with our all-state halfback, Hugh Tice, during practice. I passed out. My mother took me to our primary physician, Dr. Jay Underhill, who found I had suffered a concussion.

Dr. Jay noted that it wasn't the first time, recalling that I had been knocked out by one of my big brothers when I was three years old. It happened when they were tossing me back and forth between the edge of our backyard fishpond and an island in the middle.

"You've got to get these boys to stop playing catch with Roger," the doc said at the time during a house call.

Now, warning of the risk of future concussions, Dr. Jay advised me to give up football altogether. I shifted to cross country and track, and became the school's top miler.

Eddie Le Penske and my mother had helped inspire a love for my country. Ever since I was in junior high school, I had been interested in attending a military academy for my college education. I wanted to follow the lead of a friend and attend the US Naval Academy. But I lacked the 20/20 vision necessary for entry. My sights then turned to the US Military Academy at West Point.

Entry into West Point requires the endorsement of a member of Congress. Democratic US Sen. Warren Magnuson was the chairman of the Senate Commerce Committee when my father ran his trucking business, and they became friends. My uncle Wade, the chief executive of the California Trucking Association, called Magnuson on my behalf, and the senator remembered my father. The decision to run cross country and track also helped to gain admittance into the academy. The West Point track coach wanted me for the track team.

The summer before my senior year in high school, in 1961, I was selected to be on work crew at Malibu, the spectacular, remote camp at the entrance of a fjord in British Columbia run by the Christian group Young Life. On the bus from Seattle to Vancouver, where we were to catch a ferry, a member of the crew, Katoo Holwill, caught my eye. At a stop on the journey, I sprained my ankle in a drainage hole. I had to lay down in the back of the bus, with all the girls, and had my foot elevated on Katoo's lap from Bellingham to Vancouver. At the camp, I was given a more sedentary job, running the sports shop. Katoo worked as the head waitress in the dining hall, and we got to know each other during that month at Malibu.

Living at opposite ends of Seattle, Katoo and I didn't start dating each other until one month before our graduation from high school. I reported to West Point one month later and didn't see her for a whole year. After dating for three years from four thousand miles apart, we were engaged the summer before my Firstie (senior) year at West Point. During the fall of 1965, she moved to Highland Falls, New York, just outside the gates of West Point, on the western bank of the Hudson River north of New York City. She worked on post during my final year. Cadets are not allowed to be married until after graduation.

My class at West Point was later immortalized by author Rick Atkinson in his Pulitzer Prize-winning book "The Long Gray Line: The American Journey of West Point's Class of 1966."[1]

I entered on July 2, 1962, as one of 579 cadets who graduated in that famous class.

The "long gray line," as Atkinson put it, refers to the unique ties that bind every West Point graduate through a grueling, demanding four years that has changed little since the institution was founded in 1802.

Two US presidents, countless generals, and leaders of industry are among its graduates.

We took seriously the academy's motto, "Duty, Honor, Country." But America was on the verge of a monumental cultural shift. A classmate wrote in the early 1990s in a reunion publication: "We did not know that America would erupt into debate over every basic value in society, including the bond between country and soldier."

As a plebe, I was advised to treat everyone with respect and not burn any bridges. Someone you meet at West Point may turn out to be your commanding general, we were warned.

It turned out that the academy's superintendent during my first year was Gen. William Westmoreland. He would go on to serve as the top US Army commander in Vietnam from 1964 to 1968, overseeing the major troop buildup. He then served as Army chief of staff from 1968 to 1972.

Until his death, Westmoreland insisted the United States did not lose the war in Vietnam. Instead, he said, "our country did not fulfill its commitment to South Vietnam." Nevertheless, the US, he said, "held the line for 10 years and stopped the dominoes from falling."[2]

In his memoir, Westmoreland said that had President Lyndon B. Johnson "changed our strategy and taken advantage of the enemy's weakness to enable me to carry out the operations we had prepared over the preceding two years in Laos and Cambodia and north of the demilitarized zone, along with intensified bombing and the mining of Haiphong harbor, the North Vietnamese doubtlessly would have broken."[3]

In his view, the United States "in the end abandoned South Vietnam."

Gen. Westmoreland's daughter, Katie, was in the second grade Sunday School class that I taught. While a cadet at West Point, Westmoreland had served as superintendent of the Protestant Sunday School teachers.

I assumed that same position during my Firstie year as well.

I had direct contact with the general a couple of times. My mother got to know the general's wife, who had us over for dinner one night.

WHO LET YOU IN?

My roommate at West Point, Al Lindseth, became a lifelong friend.

Two weeks before graduation, Al and I were playing tennis, and my elbow became so sore I couldn't finish the game. I had broken it at age twelve playing football in the backyard. I went to an orthopedic doctor, but it was not set properly, and, consequently, didn't heal correctly. I wanted to play on the football team that year, so I didn't tell anybody that the elbow made a grinding noise, and it wouldn't bend beyond ninety degrees.

A cadet review parade was scheduled that afternoon on The Plain, the famous parade ground above the Hudson River. Everybody else had rifles, but the senior class, who served as officers in the cadet corps, had swords. As company commander, I issued the order, "Draw sabers!" At that moment my bad elbow locked up and I couldn't draw my saber.

I had to step out of formation and have another classmate take the company. I decided to go to the campus hospital.

When a senior walks into the hospital with a disabling injury, it's a big deal at West Point. I didn't know that. I just wanted to get my elbow fixed. It was really hurting.

Doc Ballard, the orthopedic physician, ordered x-rays. When the results arrived, the commander of the hospital, Col. Leonard, was present. The x-rays revealed the fracture that happened when I was twelve.

"Sherrard," the commander said brusquely, "did you report this when you got your physical to get into West Point?"

"Yes, sir, I did. I remember specifically. I wrote in my own hand-writing: broke elbow age twelve."

"You aren't even qualified for the draft. If you applied for the draft, you wouldn't be accepted into the Army," Leonard roared. "In fact, this might be a non-waiverable injury.

"Who in the hell gave you your physical?"

"You did, sir."

Col. Leonard was silent for an awkward moment.

Lowering his voice, he asked, "Anything else wrong with you, Sherrard?"

"Well, I have flat feet, sir," I replied.

"Let me see," he said, confirming that I indeed had no arches.

"You're not qualified for the draft on two scores!" he exclaimed.

The clinic spent the next few weeks fixing me up so I could go to Ranger school. Otherwise, I suspected, my entry into West Point would have been a big black mark on Col. Leonard's record.

Leonard investigated, and apparently somebody had taken an x-ray of my left arm—the x-rays in those days were just negatives—flipped it over and marked it as my right arm.

If I hadn't gone to West Point, none of the story I'm about to tell would have happened.

Katoo and I were married June 24, 1966, at University Presbyterian Church in Seattle, where our families lived.

We had a month-long honeymoon before I reported for Ranger School at Fort Benning, Georgia. Katoo packed up our belongings and met me there after Ranger school was finished. Then came six weeks of Airborne school before we were shipped off to Germany, north of Frankfurt.

Despite being a second lieutenant with no experience, I was a platoon leader and company commander of an armored unit with seventeen tanks. A company commander normally has three to six years of experience as an officer. But it was the Vietnam War, and we were short by one-third the manpower we needed. If that wasn't enough, all of our equipment was breaking down, and we were short of supplies.

I lost five tanks on my first maneuver, due to maintenance problems, and feared I might be relieved of command.

We were in the famous Fulda Gap, the traditional invasion route to Western Europe on the front lines of the Iron Curtain. By treaty, the Soviet army was allowed to send people to our unit to observe us while on maneuvers. We had to be very careful not to let the Soviet visitors see the position of our tanks, in case we went to war.

In the spring of 1968, I interviewed for an aide de camp position with Maj. Gen. John S. Hughes. I didn't think I had a prayer, because Hughes was an artillery general, and usually aides are chosen from the same branch of combat arms.

The general, who was Gen. George Patton's forward artillery chief during World War II, didn't tell me where we were going when he selected me. Two months later, we were moving to Italy.

In May 1968, Hughes assumed command of the United States Southern Europe Task Force (known as SETAF). He was in charge of NATO forces south of the Alps and in Turkey.

If we had gone to war in Europe, he would have assumed command over all the infantry, artillery, and frontline combat soldiers for NATO, including the Italian army.

'YOU TAKE THE BACKUP PLANE'

The general had received several inquiries from the Pentagon about reducing SETAF's personnel.

On the night of February 27, 1969, Maj. Gen. Hughes and I were to meet high-ranking officials from the Pentagon flying in from Greece to Milan's Linate Airport. We then were to fly to Livorno, Italy, about two hundred miles to the south, on the Mediterranean coast. The mission was to evaluate the impact of possible troop reductions. At the last minute, because of fog, the officials' flight was diverted from Linate to the other international airport in Milan, Malpensa.

We had two airplanes, which was protocol for a major general.

Hughes told me, "Roger, you take the backup plane to Livorno. I'll fly over to Malpensa in this plane and pick them up. Whoever gets to Livorno first, tell Colonel Smith to let the troops stand down. We'll see you in Livorno."

It was the only time I had been separated from the general on a trip.

As it lifted off from Linate Airport, the Beechcraft U-8D Seminole, carrying the general, crashed into a fence and advertising signs about three hundred yards from the end of the runway. Hughes, just fifty-two years old, and the pilot were killed.

In Livorno, the staff heard about the fatal plane crash on the news before I could get a call through to inform them. We were all in shock, consumed with deep sadness.

My main job following the crash was to help Mrs. Hughes and her four children return to the United States from Italy and get settled in a new home.

FIGHTING TYRANNY

After the death of Maj. Gen. Hughes, Maj. Gen. Robert E. Coffin—who also was an officer under Patton—took command in Northern Italy and asked me to be his aide.

The general informed me of his decision to keep me on his staff while I was helping Mrs. Hughes settle in Colorado Springs, Colorado.

He conducted an initial interview by phone then asked me to meet him in Washington, DC, before I returned to Italy.

However, he was summoned to the White House the morning I was scheduled to meet with him.

He later told me he thought he was going there in his military capacity to give a briefing. But, according to the general, an official close to newly elected President Richard Nixon was running the meeting. The official wanted a troop cut, he said, and it seemed clear that the rationale was political rather than tactical, to bolster the Republican Party.

Coffin demurred. "Gentlemen, that is a political matter, and I need to step out."

It was one of many examples of his character and integrity. Maj. Gen. Hughes also was averse to political interests overruling sound military policy. He got mad at me for registering him to vote in his home state of Oklahoma. We were trying to get everyone in the military to vote. But Hughes said he didn't vote in presidential elections, because he had to work for the winner.

Coffin hired me as his aide for three months, concluding that the phone interviews and other information were sufficient.

He said I was to get orders sooner than that to go to Vietnam, but he would cancel them.

Coffin served as the US Army's deputy chief of research and development before the assignment to Italy. During World War II, he was transferred to Gen. Patton's Armor Corps and served as counter-battery and Naval gunfire officer. He landed in Sicily with the assault forces and participated in the campaign to seize Palermo and Messina. On D-Day, he landed in Southern France, directing the fire of naval guns supporting the 7th Army, which he later joined as operations officer.

'NO ONE ELSE HAS DONE WHAT YOU'VE DONE'

On the twentieth anniversary of NATO in 1969, we had a big celebration. Katoo and I sat next to a charismatic Italian businessman, and we had an engaging conversation. He invited us to meet him the next day at Piazza Roma in Venice. He picked us up in his beautiful mahogany boat, with a little cabin in the middle. We found out he was the executive director for Northern Italy of Radiotelevisione Italiana, the state television and radio broadcaster known as Rai.

We rode to his palazzo and he took us on a tour of Venice.

"You may not know this, but I'm the president of the Venetian gastronomic society, and I'm going to take you to the best restaurant in the city," he said.

It was a little *trattoria* on the Grand Canal, not far from the Rialto Bridge. At the table, he educated us on the proper way to enjoy Italian food.

"You must always pair white wine with fish and foul," he said, "and red wine with beef or red meat."

He noted a man at the table across from us was breaking the cardinal rule, drinking red wine with fish.

"Take, for instance, that man over there," he said. "He should be taken to St. Mark's Square and shot."

"We've got to get you Americans squared away," he said, with a gleam in his eyes.

But later in our conversation, he made it clear that the evening was not about cultural or social etiquette.

"You may wonder why I invited you here to dine with me," he said.

"I wanted to show my appreciation for what your country did for us during the Second World War.

"You liberated my country from a fascist dictatorship and gave us freedom and democracy," he continued.

"The young people of Italy are not being reminded and taught this today. And I wanted someone to tell you we are thankful for what your country did.

"No other country has done what the United States has done."

ONE SMALL STEP

We stayed at the Coffins' house the last night we were in Italy, July 20,

1969, when a man landed on the moon for the first time.

My brother Jerry had asked us to purchase a red Alfa Romeo Spider convertible for him before we left Italy. We broke it in by driving it up to Norway to visit the family farm my mother's father came from in the remote fjord town of Liabygda.

When we crossed the border at the Brenner Pass into Austria, the border guards cheered, celebrating the moon landing with American citizens.

We traveled with a tent and camped the whole way. In Copenhagen, we bought tickets through the Army—at twenty-five cents each—for an Ella Fitzgerald concert at Tivoli Gardens. It was a beautiful evening, and we left the top down when we parked the Alfa Romeo on a broad street in front of the restaurant where we had dinner.

On the way back to the car at about 9 p.m., we got caught in a big thunderstorm. The exposed Alfa was on the other side of a six-lane boulevard. Not wanting it to be damaged, I raced across the road. As I tried to reach a traffic island, a car suddenly stopped in front of me. The driver of another car apparently didn't see me and grazed me, sending me to the asphalt. I picked myself up, signaling to Katoo that I was fine. But when I got to the car, I realized I couldn't move my right shoulder.

Katoo came from behind, carrying a shoe I had lost, and she put the top up on the car. We went into the restaurant to call for an ambulance. At the hospital, the doctor said my shoulder was dislocated. They worked on me for about forty-five minutes to no avail. The doctor said I would have to spend the night in the hospital. Just as he said that, I relaxed, and the arm moved back into the socket.

But I had to keep my arm strapped to my torso, so Katoo drove the rest of the way to the farm.

The injury further delayed my departure to Vietnam. By the time I was to arrive in the fall of 1969, my armor assignment was gone, and I had to take an infantry assignment instead, because they didn't have enough infantry officers. But I had qualified to be an infantry officer by graduating from Ranger school.

TAKE THAT HILL

In Vietnam, I was put in charge of the D Company, Second Battalion, First Infantry, 196th Light Infantry Brigade.

On December 2, 1969, I was flown with about fifty men to the Khe Sanh Valley, about twenty miles south of Da Nang, where we encountered immediate, massive resistance from the North Vietnamese Army.

Pinned down by enemy fire, a brutal bloodbath ensued. During the first lift, every one of our eight helicopters, transporting about half of my company, were shot down after liftoff. The man next to me was shot and killed. Eleven other soldiers in my company were killed that night.

We were surrounded by about twenty thousand North Vietnamese Army soldiers; the Viet Cong were nowhere to be seen.

I prayed, "Lord, what do I do?"

I heard a reply as clear as someone talking to me: "Take that hill."

Four or five small hills surrounded the landing zone. There was one hill from which no fire was coming. It was a North Vietnamese Army (NVA) position with fox holes around the perimeter and a machine-gun pit at the center, which they must have left to engage the helicopters. The gunners on the helicopters stripped their machine guns and ammunition from the choppers, and we all climbed the hill to position the weapons.

Once we took the hill, other troops were supposed to drive the North Vietnamese into us at the top, but no other units showed up. The NVA probed us all night, trying to find a weakness in our perimeter. With the help of a South Vietnamese Ranger battalion, we drove the NVA away.

The next morning, via a secure radio, the battalion commander informed us we were to be flown with new supplies to another landing, about twelve miles away, where we would walk another three miles to a village.

Four choppers each made two lifts to transport my men to the next landing, a dried-out rice paddy.

It's important to note here that when I had asked for resupplies, I said I needed hand grenades. But, instead, somebody sent us smoke grenades. My troops had wanted to pile them up and incinerate them, because smoke grenades are big and heavy. They're like a quart jar. I told my men we wouldn't have time to wait for them to be incinerated, so we had to carry them out. Also, we used smoke grenades to mark targets, and we didn't want the North Vietnamese to have them.

As we were traversing the rice paddy, Doc Jones, our medic, suddenly said, "Sir, look over there."

At the edge of the jungle, North Vietnamese soldiers were setting up crew-served weapons—operated by two or more people—including machine guns and bazookas.

We were sitting ducks.

Except that we each had eight smoke grenades. "Pop smoke," I ordered.

Concealed in a grayish shroud, we walked through the paddy unharmed.

"How did you know, sir?" my men asked me later.

God knew.

A PRICE ON MY HEAD

On another mission, a squad in my company discovered North Vietnamese Army documents that had been hidden in a US Army ammo can, to secure them from water and heat. Translated into English, they turned out to be orders for particular units. They included quotas for killing soldiers and shooting down helicopters.

Among the orders was a price on my head of $10,000.

The Army's policy was to remove anyone from the field who was the target of a specific threat. So, I was assigned to the Chu Lai Combat Base on the Kỳ Hà peninsula, about forty miles southeast of Da Nang. Chu Lai was the division headquarters of Marine Aircraft Group 13, known as MAG-13, where F4 Phantom jets were based.

I had the best job you could have as a captain. I ran the division operation center during the day. That meant receiving all reports of enemy contact. The reports came to staff brigade at lower headquarters, and we reported them to high command.

During this time, Gen. William Peers came to Vietnam to investigate the My Lai massacre. Lt. William Calley had been charged with premeditated murder in the death of 109 Vietnamese civilians in March 1968. We had to secure the village, identified as My Lai 4, before the investigative team arrived. The 48th battalion of the Viet Cong, the South Vietnamese resistance aligned with the communist north, had its headquarters just above My Lai 4.

I received from the field the reports of casualties we took to secure the village. And I gave the briefing every night of enemy contact in the division. It was a one-hundred-mile area, from Da Nang to the pass leading to the central highlands.

Maj. Gen. Albert E. Milloy, commander of the First Infantry Division, was named on March 22, 1970, to take over command of the American Division.

Milloy frequently teased me for being an armor officer rather than an infantry officer.

"What are we doing with an armor officer giving the briefing to the staff every night?"

During World War II, Milloy saw combat action as a paratrooper in the Battle of the Bulge with the 504th Parachute Infantry Regiment, one of the nation's most decorated units. In Korea, as commander of the 2nd Battalion, 3rd Regiment, he led his men through the Chinese spring offensive, the "Punch Bowl," and "Heartbreak Ridge." After an initial tour in Vietnam in 1965, he returned in 1969 to command the 1st Infantry Division.

Milloy had taken over command of the American Division in Vietnam from Maj. Gen. Lloyd B. Ramsey five days after Ramsey was seriously injured in a crash of his command helicopter in Viet Cong-controlled territory.

Ramsey had been my division commander in Germany. He was awarded five Purple Hearts during World War II before helping the 3rd Infantry Division reach Austria, where it liberated Salzburg and captured Adolf Hitler's retreat in nearby Berchtesgaden, Germany.

CONTENTIOUS CLASSROOM

I believed I was in Vietnam to help stop the tide of communism and save the Vietnamese people from tyranny.

While I was deployed, Katoo was studying art at the University of Washington. She had a visiting professor from New York City for her oil painting class. At the beginning of winter quarter, she had to ask permission to leave a week early before finals to meet me for much-needed R and R in Hawaii.

She told the professor stories of my unit helping villagers harvest their rice. In one instance, I helped a Mr. Toi harvest his rice for the first time in twenty years. The communists had prevented him from taking it to the market.

All during that quarter at the university, the professor argued with Katoo about the Vietnam War. He didn't believe the stories.

NOT MANY LEFT LIKE THAT

I resigned from the Army in 1970. Gen. Roy Atteberry—whom I was serving with for a second time—happened to be stationed in Worms, Germany when I became aide de camp for Gen. Hughes. Katoo's sister was Gen. Atteberry's secretary there. He saw my resignation and wanted to know the reason.

I told him I had been asked to "change" the figures on a report to headquarters and I couldn't do it.

After a rocket attack one morning on the Chu Lai base, we reported we had been hit by a total of 239 Russian 122-millimeter rockets. The figures were derived from men actually counting rocket-launching stakes and backblast marks.

At the conference in which I gave the report, the commanding general stood up and said, "I don't believe that."

Clearly, an attack of 239 rockets didn't make him look good.

"I stood on my hootch," the general said, "and there were not more than forty rockets that hit our base camp."

Forty clearly was a much more manageable number for his success.

I believe the spot report got changed to forty, but I don't know that for sure.

In any case, I told Gen. Atteberry I had been asked to change a report and couldn't do it.

During World War II, Atteberry was a major on Gen. Dwight Eisenhower's staff. He was asked to do a study and give a report to the supreme allied commander on how to maintain the best junior officers in the Army.

Atteberry presented the report to Eisenhower in his office, with the general's full coterie present. Ike didn't like the report. Upset, Atteberry walked out and shut the glass door behind him a little harder than usual. Glass fell to the floor, and Atteberry stopped.

Eisenhower barked, "Don't pick it up. We'll take care of it. Get out of here, major."

Later, at the officer's club, Atteberry was drinking his beer alone. Thinking his Army career was finished, he thought, "What am I going to do?"

Somebody put a hand on his shoulder. It was Ike. The five-star general said, "I was a little brusque with you this afternoon, and I apologize."

Atteberry told me, "Roger, there aren't too many people left in the Army like that, I'm sorry to say. I understand what you're doing."

He didn't argue with me about my resignation.

However, the Army didn't accept my resignation, and we were assigned to Fort Jackson in South Carolina.

After serving at Fort Jackson for two and a half years, we finally left the Army. It was not an easy decision. But Katoo and I prayed and asked God for wisdom, and it was clear that I should get out.

I had taken the LSAT, the Law School Admission Test, just before leaving Vietnam in preparation for applying to law schools.

On my last day in the Army, Maj. Gen. Robert Charles Hixon took over command of Fort Jackson. My brother, Dr. Don Sherrard, had served in Germany under Hixon, a battalion commander, while I was a cadet at West Point. Don was the battalion physician for three years.

My brother never liked the Army, and he even had offered to pay my way to another university rather than go to West Point.

Gen. Hixon was aware of this, but he had a favorable view of Don when he called me into his office that last day.

"Captain Sherrard, if you want to stay in the Army, we can get your resignation purged," he said. "Five years, you can go anywhere you want to go. No one will know you resigned."

I told him I didn't want to be a divorced person in the Army.

3

MERCY FOR THOSE

WHO GIVE MERCY

IN SEPTEMBER 1972, after taking an admissions test while still in Vietnam, I entered law school at the University of Puget Sound. Later, the law school was taken over by Seattle University, which awarded me my degree.

During my final year of law school, I worked for the Pierce County prosecutor's office on traffic and misdemeanor cases. We handled many misdemeanor marijuana cases, and there was an unspoken deal with the prosecutor that if the accused didn't have any law violations for a year after the incident, we would drop charges. It encouraged the violators to stay clean, we believed.

On my last day, we went out to lunch with the judge and a state trooper.

After leaving the restaurant, the judge got into my car in the passenger seat. Doreen Oswald, the court clerk, and the state trooper got into the back seat.

"I didn't know you smoked," she said as she held up a marijuana roach.

My whole life passed before me. A friend had been in the back seat the night before when we attended a graduation party for my law class.

I deployed all the excuses I had heard in court, including, "I didn't know that was there," which was the truth.

Their conclusion: He had been merciful, so we will be merciful.

I took the bar exam and passed.

HARVEST TIME

After law school I began interviewing with big firms in Seattle. A partner of one of the firms invited us for dinner at a beautiful home on Lake Washington. I was told that if you get invited for dinner, you're on the short list. The joke in law school was that when you get that opportunity, don't spill dinner on the wrong person at the wrong time.

When we got in the car after dinner, Katoo and I looked at each other and said, "It's just like the Army, this unit." Nearly all the reasons we got out of the Army came up during the evening, and we decided we didn't want to go to a big law firm in Seattle.

My brother Jean and Bill McGonagle, a classmate of Katoo's at Roosevelt High School in Seattle, were practicing law together on Bainbridge Island, and they offered me a job.

We settled in Poulsbo, where our second son, Toby, was born in 1977.

In 1985, Katoo and I were discussing with the boys the Old Testament concept of giving a tithe—10 percent—of the harvest of grain. I asked what the equivalent was of my "grain" harvest.

Our oldest son, twelve-year-old Wade, said, without hesitation, "time."

I began to "tithe" my time by blocking off Friday afternoons, 10 percent of my work week. But I soon realized that this was not my "first fruit" but rather my "last fruit." By Friday afternoon I was tired. And so, I began to block out Monday mornings.

In the summer of 1985, the pastor of my church, Al Munger, asked me and a physician who also was a church member, Bob Bethel, to give public talks on the medical and legal aspects of abortion.

We spoke at the Rotary and Lions Clubs as well as at churches.

One January night, I received a telephone call from a fireman in Tacoma, Ed Kramer, who had lost a trial court case for criminal trespass of a doctor's office where he and others were protesting abortion. A trial judge had found them guilty, and he wanted a trial lawyer to help them appeal.

I had some trial experience by that time. But I didn't have experience in constitutional law. In the meantime, while I sorted out what to do, I put in a notice of appearance in Ed's case so that nothing bad would happen to him without me being notified.

I found out he had been given only ten days to file an answer to a complaint in the court of appeals. By then, only seven days were left. I was unable to find a suitable lawyer for him. So, I had to submit an answer to the court myself.

I knew that as a lawyer, political cases such as this one could brand you for life. But I was stuck. Once you submit an answer, you can't get out of it.

The brief was due in September, and I would then argue in court in November.

BEYOND THE SEA

At that time, Bob and I were still getting invitations to speak. I debated a University of Washington constitutional law professor in Port Angeles, in the far northwest corner of Washington state. I argued that the Roe v. Wade opinion written by Justice Harry Blackmon had no constitutional basis. His reply, after the debate, was that I was just one of those "Bible thumpers."

Meanwhile, a lawyer in Poulsbo, Jeff Tolman, came up with the idea to launch a continuing legal education seminar hosted by local attorneys. For the first three annual seminars, they had managed to get legendary criminal defense attorneys Richard "Racehorse" Haynes and Gerry Spence, and US Supreme Court Associate Justice Antonin Scalia as keynote speakers. The seminar was developing quite a reputation, and it became a very well attended event. Now they were working on inviting US Supreme Court Associate Justice John Paul Stevens.

Washington State Supreme Court Justice Bob Utter was helping to host Stevens and wanted to take him out on his ocean racing sailboat. Utter called me, saying he had heard I knew how to sail. He asked me and Katoo to help as crew for the day. Many of the sitting state Supreme Court justices were invited as well as my former West Point roommate, Al Lindseth, and his wife, Carroll, who were visiting us.

We spent the whole afternoon with Justice Stevens and became friends with the Utters on that outing.

I didn't know it at the time, but while I was sailing with Stevens, the Kramer case was kicked up to the state Supreme Court by a motion of the Court of Appeals. It was to be joined with four other cases from around the state.

Suddenly, it became a huge story.

That fall, every newspaper in the state covered our case with a very negative slant. To my knowledge, it was the first case of any significance about abortion demonstrators to reach the court of appeals or the Supreme Court in the state of Washington.

At that point I was a little stressed out.

On three successive days, I had a clear impression during my time of prayer that I should contact Ken Vanderhoef, a lawyer in downtown Seattle. He had argued before the US Supreme Court in the Roe v. Wade case on behalf of the Roman Catholic Church.

On the fourth day, I called him.

He said, "I've been waiting for you to call. Come on over. I don't have any appointments until eleven."

After presenting the cases to him, his simple advice was don't talk about abortion or doctor's offices.

He looked at his watch, and it almost eleven o'clock.

I walked out of the Norton building back to the ferry thinking what a waste of time that was.

While riding back on the ferry, I sat down and pulled out the next case file that my secretary, Linda Wood, had given me. It was NAACP vs. Claiborne Hardware. Suddenly, Ken's comment made sense. Blacks in the South were arrested for demonstrating against a store that wouldn't hire them. The opinion was written by John Paul Stevens. It had been cited in several of our briefs.

As I started reading it, I realized it was our case. The only difference was that it was a hardware store, not an abortion clinic, and the issue was civil rights, not abortion.

Before returning to the Poulsbo office, I stopped at our firm's Bainbridge Island office to talk about it with my partners, Bill and my brother Jean. They agreed this was a divinely inspired strategy.

'DO YOU KNOW THE ANSWER TO MY QUESTION?'

At the Washington State Supreme Court, supporters of the National Organization for Women, NOW, filled the gallery.

Katoo recalled later that as she was asking God how to pray, Old Testament scriptures came to mind about how Israel won battles against great odds when God brought confusion to the enemy camp.

The media, all the newspapers and television news departments, backed the abortion defenders.

I felt totally oppressed. I went to the library to pray and collect my thoughts, and walked back.

The clerk told me I was ten minutes late. They had drawn straws to determine the order in which the five lawyers would argue, and I was to go last.

Associate Justice Robert F. Brachtenbach interrupted the first lawyer, from the ACLU, after he had gotten out only a sentence.

"What if this were not an abortion clinic?" the justice asked. "What if it were a wood-stove store and the protesters were protesting carcinogens that poison the air?"

The ACLU lawyer, apparently confused by the question, replied, "This is about abortion, your honor, this is not about wood stoves."

The justice posed the question to all four ACLU attorneys, and none had an answer.

When my turn came, Brachtenbach, who served a total of twenty-two years on the high court, asked, "Mr. Sherrard, do you know the answer to my question?"

"Yes, I do," I said, citing Stevens' opinion in NAACP vs. Claiborne Hardware.

"Freedom of speech to express political thought is the highest rung on the ladder of free speech," I said.

The ACLU lawyers walked out with their heads down.

Wade, my twelve-year-old, came up to me after the hearing, "Dad, you blew them away."

We won 9-0 at the Supreme Court.

But there was not one word in the papers. After constant coverage that fall and a full contingent of reporters at the hearing, the result apparently was not newsworthy.

Nevertheless, I became an instant "expert" on constitutional law, representing many people who had been found guilty in trial court for protesting abortion clinics. We never lost a case on that issue.

In my view, the ACLU lawyers essentially argued: This is about abortion, which trumps the rule of law and the freedom of speech.

But the rule of law prevails over opinions and political agendas.

As much as that concept shocks the sensibilities of some activists and legal minds in the United States, it's a completely alien concept in most of the world. And post-communist Eastern Europe certainly was no exception.

4

PREPARED IN ADVANCE

"For we are God's handiwork, created in Christ Jesus to do good works, which God prepared in advance for us to do." EPHESIANS 2:10

MY INTRODUCTION TO POST-COMMUNIST EUROPE began in another Balkan nation, Bulgaria. On the Black Sea, between Romania and Greece, it was the fourth nation to catch the revolutionary wave of 1989 that began in Poland.

In 1990, the Bulgarian Parliament officially revoked the "leading role" the Communist Party had held for more than four decades. The people of a nation that was once the Soviet Union's closest ally now had to figure out how to govern themselves.

I learned from Art Moore, after he visited Sofia in early 1991, of the need for Western legal minds to help Bulgaria establish a rule of law. American law experts had helped write the constitution. But Bulgarian lawyers wanted help understanding and implementing fundamental principles such as liberty, freedom of expression, and human rights. And they needed practical knowledge, such as how to run a law practice.

The next day, I called Sam Ericsson, who had helped me with my legal briefs in the Washington State Supreme Court case. Sam had just resigned as the director of the Christian Legal Society, because he wanted to pursue invitations from Russia to help lawyers and churches transition to a free society.

"You called me on the first day I haven't had a job since I graduated from Harvard Law School," Sam said.

He was at home contemplating how the Lord was going to lead him next.

I told him of the need in Bulgaria, hoping to pass the invitation to him. I reasoned that it was not the task for a business and estate planning lawyer from Poulsbo. Sam said he needed time to pray about how he should be involved.

Within minutes, he called back to tell me that upon hanging up the phone, he received a call from a Bulgarian who had known his parents in Sweden. Like Sam's parents, the Bulgarian also emigrated to the United States. Sam took pride in having been born in Sweden, where he lived until age five.

The Bulgarian who called Sam also was looking for a Christian lawyer to go to his native country and help with the legal system. After two phone calls, just minutes apart, Sam was ready to sign up. But he would not let me back out of the request.

"You're just the guy," he said. "You worked for the government and argued and won a case before the Washington State Supreme Court."

We decided to make an exploratory trip together in July 1991. I received a handwritten fax from our initial contact, University of Sofia law student Radoslav Kotorov, asking us to confirm the dates of our visit.

"You should know that our country is in deep economic crisis and your help will be very beneficial to the development of the democratic process," Kotorov wrote in conclusion.

Bill Larsen, a law professor in Los Angeles, joined us on the trip to Sofia as well, bringing along a library of 1,100 case-law books. We packed them in several sport bags, and we weren't charged for extra luggage when airline agents learned of our mission.

We arrived in the wake of a controversial election that had replaced one-third of the seats with pro-democracy party members after five decades of single-party communist rule. The Parliament had just approved a new constitution.

Radoslav arrived at the airport to meet us in his 1961 Dodge Comet and showed us to our apartment. We were immediately jarred by the custom, also practiced in Albania, of shaking the head to signify a yes response and nodding to indicate no.

"You're taking us to our apartment? No? Yes? Maybe?"

Along the way, we saw thousands protesting in the streets, shouting anti-communist slogans and waving the blue flags of the Union of Democratic Forces.

On the radio, the hit songs bore titles such as "Communism, I want a Divorce" and "Communism Go Away."

Bulgaria's Communist Party seized power during World War II. By October 1944, according to Central Intelligence Agency documents, 26,850 people were killed by the government without court sentences.[4] By December of that year, the regime had installed special People's Courts authorized to prosecute "fascists," a term applied to anyone who had opposed the communists.

Todor Zhivkov, appointed Communist Party general secretary in 1956, remained in power until one day after the Berlin Wall fell on November 9, 1989. His brutal rule was characterized by perhaps the closest relationship with Moscow of any of the Soviet satellites in Eastern Europe.

WHERE DO OUR RIGHTS COME FROM?

Shortly after our afternoon arrival, we met with Anton Antonov, the chairman of Bulgaria's bar association, called the Central Council of Solicitors. Then it was on to the Parliament and a meeting with the secretary, Emilia Droumeva.

With briefcases in hand, we exited the Parliament building to head to the University of Sofia law school. Outside Parliament, a massive crowd had gathered. An overturned car was on fire. News people were all over the place.

We didn't know it—we were merely choosing the most direct route to the law school—but we had just passed through a picket line demonstrating against the government.

At the law school, we were met by the dean, Slavi Pachovski. The contact with dean Pachovski came through the Bulgarian who had made the second call asking Sam to go and help. The emigre and the dean, as well as the assistant dean, were good friends.

Pachovski, who later became Bulgaria's ambassador to the United Nations, hosted about forty students who were in their fifth year of law school in 1991. They had entered in 1986 under a communist regime.

At that moment, the Parliament was considering a human-rights bill.

"Isn't it great that Parliament is considering giving us human rights?" one of the students declared.

"No, it's not great," I replied.

You could have heard a pin drop.

Finally, a student spoke. "Why do you think that?"

"If Parliament thinks it can give you your human rights today, it can take them away tomorrow," I explained.

A student interjected, "I know where that idea comes from. Your Declaration of Independence. We are endowed by our creator with certain unalienable rights."

I was curious to know how he knew about the Declaration of Independence, and he responded, "We studied it as a revolutionary document in communist theory class.»

That night, the television news reported that visiting American constitutional lawyers had braved the picket line to go to the law school.

Slavi later explained to us that our crossing the picket line ensured that nobody would vote against the human rights bill.

'PEACE' ABOVE ALL

In Sofia, we dined with Anton Antonov, the Bulgarian bar president, along with a man, in his 60s, regarded as the best lawyer in Bulgaria.

The lawyer said he was ashamed that his generation did not stand up against the Soviet Union and the government it imposed on his nation when he launched his career.

"My generation gave up the right to freedom. We wanted peace more than anything. They knew that's what we wanted, and they gave it to us," he said.

His confession recalled to my mind Benjamin Franklin's famous quote: "Those who would give up essential liberty, to purchase a little temporary safety, deserve neither liberty nor safety."

Antonov observed that the essential conflict is not "a war with guns and swords, but a war of ideas."

By the 1980s, the Soviet Union had lost that war of ideas, and its empire was held together only by guns and swords—its military.

Antonov saw a relationship between the display of US power during the first Gulf War from August 1990 to February 1991 and the dissolution of the Soviet Union on December 26, 1991.

"We watched on CNN and saw how the American-trained military was far superior to the Soviets. We knew that that glue wouldn't hold anymore," he told us.

"We watched what the American Air Force did to Soviet equipment in Iraq," said Anton, whose brother was in the Bulgarian Air Force. "They decimated the Soviet army."

While attending my twenty-fifth class reunion at West Point, in 1991, we learned more fascinating facts about the Gulf War that were never reported. During a breakfast meeting, a brigadier general recalled having his troops positioned in Kuwait, just across the border from Iraq. They were prepared at first light to be one of the first units to invade. He felt compelled to pray with some of his men for God to go before them. That night, a strong wind arose, followed by torrents of rain. They were puzzled by the unusual weather, but at dawn, as they approached the minefields they had to cross to invade Iraq, it all became clear.

The wind and rain had miraculously exposed the mines, and they passed through with zero casualties. They also were surprised, when they initially engaged with the enemy, to find that none of the Iraqi tanks were firing on them. It turned out that the ocular devices on the Iraqis' Russian-made tanks had fogged up because of the moisture from the rain.

Seven years later, in 1998, the impact of American military might was seen in Kosovo, the Serbian province with an ethnic Albanian majority.

My West Point classmate Gen. Wes Clark took command of NATO, which carried out the controversial bombing of the Serbian regime of Slobodan Milosevic. Wes, like many in the international community, believed the Serbians were preparing to carry out genocide against the ethnic Albanians in Kosovo, which the Serbs considered their ancient homeland.

In any case, it was clear what neighboring Albania thought about America's action.

In Tirana, a large banner hung across a main street saying, "Thank you, NATO. Thank you, United States."

PRAY FOR BULGARIA

During our time in Bulgaria, I became intrigued by a song played regularly on the radio by the opposition party, the Union of Democratic Forces, which was founded in 1989 as a coalition of several political organizations in opposition to the communist government.

The chorus of the song, which became the nation's most popular, went, "Pray for Bulgaria. God grant my Bulgaria a way of light and liberty."

I had hoped to meet the man behind the song, Boyan Popov, the party's minister of communications, but couldn't make it work.

Sam flew to London, and I boarded a flight to Zurich.

Someone was sitting in my seat on the Bulgarian Airlines Tupolev 134 jet.

"Who are you?" the man asked me.

"I'm Roger Sherrard, an American lawyer," I replied.

"Oh, I wanted to meet you," the man said.

"Who are you?" I asked.

"I am Boyan Popov, the government's minister of communications."

We became friends, and Boyan and his wife stayed at our home in Poulsbo on a trip to the United States. They brought us two beautiful, framed porcelain relief tiles. One was of the crucified Christ.

FOR SUCH A TIME AS THIS

Before separating at the airport in Sofia, Sam and I reflected on our visit.

"When, since the time of Saint Paul, have lawyers been able to be missionaries and have such influence on governments?" he asked.

The biblical story of Esther came up in our discussions. We adopted chapter 4, verse 13 as the theme for this nation-building work: "And who knows but that you have come to royal position for such a time as this?"

Our mutual interest led to the formation one year later of Advocates International, and Sam Ericsson became its first director. Building on Sam's years of international travel and extraordinary ability to network and engage with people, the organization now has some thirty thousand local advocates "doing justice with compassion" on every continent.

On March 24, 1992, I was working late one night in my Poulsbo office with John Davies, a lawyer from Alaska who was helping us set up our computer system. It was about 6:15 p.m., and we thought that we heard the front door open. We both wondered if we had forgotten to lock the door and someone had come in. I went and checked, and the door was locked. We both suspected someone had come in and might have been hiding in one of the offices.

John looked down the north side of the building, and I looked down the south side, and we ended up together at the fax machine as it beeped on.

There was a letter sitting in the fax tray already. And another one was coming in.

I picked up the letter from the fax tray. It was from Art Moore, a client and a longtime family friend, who was living in Vienna, Austria.

I glanced over it, and it said in essence, "Could you put together a team of lawyers and judges to go to Albania?"

The second letter was from Mark Spengler, the vice chancellor of the University of the Nations in Kona, Hawaii. It said, "Could you put together a team of lawyers and judges to go to Albania?"

Mark and Art did not know each other.

Spengler, whom I had never met, opened his letter recalling that the book of Esther "tells a story about a young lady who God had prepared to perform a strategic role in the furtherance of his plans for the Jewish people." He concluded his opening paragraph with the words "for such a time as this."

But I wasn't convinced. I was focused on Bulgaria. I'm not a guy that jumps from one thing to the other. But God knew that. So, as he often does, he sent me a "two-by-four" to get my attention.

Mel Hosel, a businessman from Everett, heard I had been to Bulgaria and wanted to meet with me. He was planning to set up an import-export business to import crafts and other items into the US from Bulgaria. He called me the next morning and said, "I don't usually do this, but I want to change the subject, to Albania, not Bulgaria."

He had just returned from the Balkans and had visited Albania.

"I don't know why, but I have to show you this film from Albania; they have far greater needs there," he said.

WHY ME?

The Albanians wanted an American lawyer who knew something about constitutional law and had not worked for a large corporation or the government.

That's almost humorous. You couldn't have found a more obscure law office in America. They didn't know that. But no one else was responding. And as a small-town lawyer, when there's a need, you meet it.

Sam and I had returned to Bulgaria in March 1992 to serve as election monitors and planned another trip in July 1992 to hold a multi-day seminar for lawyers. We tacked on a trip to Albania.

In Bulgaria, we visited the office of the minister of justice in Sofia. We were accompanied by Mimi Antonova, the daughter of bar president Anton Antonov.

During our meeting with judicial officials, Mimi suddenly began crying and ran out of the room. I went after her to see what was going on.

"I just became overwhelmed being in that office," she explained, "because many people were sentenced to death there, and I couldn't take it anymore."

Exhausted after three days in Bulgaria, we hopped aboard a Balkan Air Tupolev 34 jet for Tirana, Albania. The route was not direct, due to the war in Serbia. We couldn't fly over Macedonia, which had gained independence from Yugoslavia in 1991.

Curiously, the smoking section of our jetliner was on the left side of the aisle and the non-smoking on the right. A little sign in English above our seats in a rectangular opening notified us of an escape rope stored inside.

We landed in Tirana, where our luggage was put on a donkey cart for a short trip to the tiny terminal. There, it was pushed through an opening in a wall, where we retrieved it.

We stayed at the home of Nico and Lillian Mirdita. Their house had been in the family for generations before it was seized by the communist regime shortly after World War II, and it had only recently been returned to them. It was a single-family home, which was unusual in the capital city. They rented rooms for $10 a night per person, with breakfast, which was about one-fifth the average monthly wage at the time.

Lillian told us that during the communist era, she hid a crucifix in sheets in her linen closet. She would get it out at night to pray, when the children were asleep, because she didn't want them to see it. She knew the consequence of it being discovered could be ten to forty years in prison.

At the Mirditas', I got a taste of the economic chaos that followed the fall of the communist regime.

Amid severe food shortages, the water was on only in the middle of the night, and electric power frequently failed. If you wanted luxuries that we take for granted at home, such as a shower, you had to get up at 3 a.m.

SOMETHING TO BELIEVE IN

My visit took place just one year after hopes had been raised among Albanians that America would save the nation with a "Marshall Plan."

In June 1991 some three hundred thousand euphoric Albanians chanting "USA! USA!" filled Tirana's Skanderbeg Square to greet US Secretary of State James Baker. It was the first visit ever by a senior American official.

The New York Times described the scene as Baker arrived: "Hands reached out from every direction to touch the Secretary of State or to pound on the windows of his car.[5] Albanians kissed the hood and windows and showered the car with flower petals, and one man threw himself in front of the limousine and kissed the road—anything to make a link with the representative of America."

The Times said it was "as though his visit had provided the first tangible proof that their long national nightmare was over."

"Welcome to the company of free men and women everywhere, the way our Creator intended us to be," Baker told the crowd. "You are with us, and we are with you."

However, Ilir Ikonomi, a Tirana Radio correspondent, told the Times that now that "the communists are almost gone, this country is going through a crisis of faith" and their expectations are unrealistic.

"People desperately want something to believe in and they really believe that America will solve all our problems. People have been looking forward to this day, but I think they are placing too much hope in America. Their hopes are exaggerated," he said.

Baker was stunned by the reception, having never seen anything like it in his years in politics. He later addressed a special session of the Albanian Parliament and met with opposition leaders, including future president Sali Berisha.

Berisha recounted the meeting to the Times: "We said to Mr. Baker that we killed Communism, but we are faced with its debris which is still toxic."

Albania, Berisha explained, "has a democratic head, a democratic heart but a Bolshevik body."

The next spring, Berisha—a former personal physician for the late dictator Enver Hoxha—was elected as president in the nation's first free election.

THE BLOOD-TAX REVOLT

The archetype of Albanian character was the leader of the major revolt against the Ottoman Turkish Empire prior to its rule of the Balkans, Gjergj Kastrioti, known as Skanderbeg.[6]

Born in 1405, Skanderbeg was a member of a Christian noble family. Under the Ottomans' implementation of Islamic law, Christian families were required to pay a "blood tax," or "tribute in blood," called *devshirme* in Albanian.[7]

The Ottomans sent military officers to take Christian boys aged eight to eighteen in the Balkans from their families to be raised to serve the state. Skanderbeg was educated by the Ottoman sultan and served in the Turkish leader's house for twenty years.

But like Moses, whose royal Egyptian upbringing trained and positioned him to free the Israelites from tyranny, Skanderbeg turned his privileged Ottoman upbringing against his oppressors.

After rising through the Ottoman ranks, becoming a governor in 1440, he deserted the Ottomans and led a rebellion against the empire in what is today Albania and Macedonia. In 1444, he was appointed the chief commander of the League of Lezhë, which consolidated nobility throughout what is today Northern Albania.

For the first time, Albanians of different regions and dialects were united under a single leader in a common cause, helping define their ethnic identity.

Skanderbeg's military skills were an obstacle to Ottoman expansion. Later, many Western Europeans regarded him as a model of resistance against the Islamic empire, which was exemplified in the pivotal Battle of Vienna in 1683. For twenty-five years, Skanderbeg's ten-thousand man army won battle after battle against the much larger and better equipped Turkish forces.

It was a mosquito that eventually took down the great Skanderbeg; he contracted malaria and died in 1468 at the age of sixty-two. A little more than a decade later, in 1789, the Albanian city of Shkodra fell to the Ottomans. The Albanians revolted again in 1481, but the Ottomans finally controlled Albania by 1488.

In the sixteenth and seventeenth centuries, the Ottomans imposed Islam on the Catholic and Orthodox populations. Many Christians were said to have maintained their faith in secret in their homes while identifying as Muslim in public.

Generations later, their ancestors would adopt a similar posture under a communist regime that demanded public declarations and demonstrations of unbridled loyalty.

5

SETTING A TABLE

ON OUR FIRST TRIP TO TIRANA, we met with members of the Supreme Court and with the speaker of parliament, Pjeter Arbnori, who had been a political prisoner under the communist regime for twenty-eight years.

Arbnori also was the vice president, the first in line if something happened to Berisha. The country at the time was functioning under an interim constitution adopted in early 1992.

Under Albania's parliamentary system, the president is the head of state, representing the unity of the Albanian people in the country and abroad as the head of state. The president also is the commander-in-chief of the military. The prime minister, a deputy in the Parliament, is appointed by the party that wins a majority of seats in a popular election, or, with a plurality of seats, forms a governing coalition.

In April of 1992, Arbnori opened the first session of Parliament.

"The great honor to declare open the proceedings of the first post-war democratic parliament,» he said, "belongs not only to me but to all democrats who have suffered in jails, internment and emigration, to all the persecuted, to all the martyrs of the darkest period our homeland has lived with."

Arbnori was intimately familiar with suffering.[8] When he was seven, his father was killed fighting Enver Hoxha's partisans during World War II, which prevented him from going to college. He managed to earn a degree from the University of Tirana using fake documents and taught literature at a school in the city of Kavajë. He helped form a pro-pluralist movement that drew the attention of Albania's secret police, the Sigurimi, and he was arrested with six other colleagues. Arbnori's trial, which included lengthy interrogations and torture, lasted two years, and he was sentenced to death. Authorities commuted his sentence to twenty-five years of imprisonment, hoping he could help them arrest other leaders of the movement. Nearing the end of his sentence, he was sentenced to another ten years, but he was released in 1989. Less than five months later, he joined the anti-communist movement and participated in a demonstration in Shkodra that overturned a statue of Stalin.

At our meeting, Arbnori was accompanied by his counsel, Perikli Zaharia, and Zaharia's assistant, Vjollca Proni.

Perikli, or Peri, as we called him, later told us that during the Hoxha era, he often would go to the library to read the only American magazine available, National Geographic. He didn't want to be seen reading it all the time, so he would check out a book and hide the magazine inside. Hoxha told his people at that time that Albania was the world's most prosperous nation, regularly flashing on television bleak images of the United States during the Great Depression.

Peri said he was most fascinated by National Geographic's advertisements. They gave him a very different picture of America than the one he got from the dictator and his teachers.

At our meeting, Arbnori expressed the country's mixed feelings of elation and disorientation as the people were suddenly overwhelmed with the prospect of governing themselves.

"The West is setting a banquet before us, and we don't know which foods to eat or in which order to eat them," he told us.

They needed guidance and structure, as no one but the communists had been given any authority. Only the communists knew how to turn the water or the electricity on and off.

We asked him to tell us his greatest need.

"We don't know how to dialogue. We're not getting along, and I'm embarrassed to say that many of our disputes end up in fistfights out in the streets," he replied.

I thought to myself that I wished I had had legislative experience and could give him some practical principles. Then it occurred to me: just give him the Golden Rule.

I tried to state it in a way that is easily translatable: treat others the way you want to be treated.

Arbnori—who while in prison secretly wrote novels and short stories in code that were smuggled out—started making diagrams on paper. He wrote down what I was saying, asking me to repeat it.

"This is a universal rule," he said. "It applies government to government, government to citizen, citizen to citizen. If we followed this rule, it would solve the world's problems."

One of the country's biggest current problems, he said, was that people didn't know whom they could trust. No one would admit to having cooperated with the communists.

Many people turned in their neighbors, friends, and relatives to the police for such "subversive" activities as listening to Radio Free Europe, which was punished by a prison sentence. Complaining about the government-issued bread was considered treasonous.

From 1946 to 1991, tens of thousands of Albanians were imprisoned or sent to labor camps on political charges, and an estimated six thousand were executed, according to the country's Association of Former Political Prisoners.[9] The nation's borders were encased with electric fences and anyone trying to escape could face execution.

The secret police, the Sigurimi, established a vast surveillance network of one thousand agents and eleven thousand informants equipped with listening bugs and hidden cameras. Bugs even were placed in clothing, shoes, and bags. And close friends and relatives could turn out to be Sigurimi informants, as was documented when secret police files were finally opened to the public in 2017.

Unlike other post-communist nations, Albania didn't engage in a policy of "lustration," the purging of government officials who committed crimes in their collaboration with the old regime. Only a small number were put on trial, and few were convicted.

"So, we didn't know who the informants were. Everyone denies it, because they would have to pay a price," Arbnori said.

The problem, when it comes to choosing new leaders, the speaker explained, is "that nobody is expected to tell the truth about themselves."

"How do we know who we can trust?" he asked.

I suggested crafting an application for candidates for political office like we have in Washington state, where making false statements under oath is subject to punishment. I had reviewed several such statements for politicians, including Washington gubernatorial candidate Ellen Craswell.

The candidate's information, I said, should be submitted under penalty of perjury.

"Perjury?"

I explained that if you lie under oath, and it's proven, there is a criminal penalty.

I asked my Poulsbo law office colleague John Johnson to fax a copy of Washington state's perjury laws to the speaker's fax machine, the only fax machine in Parliament. We used up all the paper in their machine.

The lawmakers soon adopted the laws.

Later, I read an English translation of Albanian law. When I came to the perjury section, I thought to myself, this sounds very familiar.

I later learned that under the subjugation of the Ottoman Turkish empire, deceit was a way of life for Albanians. It was common for Christians, for example, to identify as Muslims in public while maintaining their faith in the privacy of their homes.

That generational practice of dual identity also became a tool of survival under communist rule.

PAPER PLEASE

We went on to the Supreme Court building and had a two-and-a-half hour meeting with the chief justice and some of the judges.

Sam asked the chief justice, "What is your greatest need?"

"Paper on which to write decisions," he replied.

When we returned home, the Washington State Bar Association immediately sent more than six hundred reams of paper. With reimbursement from the State Department, we also sent them ten computers and made the machines compatible with our computers at home, which at that time was an issue.

Our quick response gave us credibility. We didn't wait for the bar association's board of governors to vote on it. We just did it.

The chief justice asked us to come back and put on a judicial seminar for Albania's judges.

They were eager to learn from a nation with more than two centuries of rule by the people. But Albania has a long-tested system of law of its own that preceded communist rule, known as *Kanuni i Lekë Dukagjinit*, or *The Code of Lekë Dukagjini*.

Our hosts were delighted that we brought them copies of a volume that had been published in New York, with Albanian and English text side by side. *The Code of Lekë* is a compilation of laws governing personal and social conduct as well as civil and criminal matters that originated in the fifteenth century in Northern Albania, surviving communism as well as centuries of Islamic Ottoman Turkish rule.

It sheds light on the extraordinary displays of hospitality, honor, and respect I was accorded.

The cornerstone of the code is the concept of *besa*, personal honor and fidelity, and *nderi*, family honor. Etymologically, besa is related to the classical Latin word *fides*, which early Christian adopted as the word for "faith."

Common sayings related to besa include *Besa e shqiptarit si purteka e arit*, meaning "the Albanians' honor is worth more than gold." Another is *Shqiptarët vdesin dhe besen nuk e shkelin*, or "Albanians would die rather than break honor."

During the 1930s and early 1940s, besa was on display as Albanians saved an estimated six hundred to eighteen hundred Jews from Nazi persecution.[10] Instead of hiding them in attics or basements, the families gave them Albanian names and treated them as part of the family.

Some authors have conjectured that the code may derive from tribal laws of ancient Illyria, the area mentioned by the Apostle Paul in Romans 15:19 as part of his missionary travels.

The code evolved as it was passed on over the centuries orally through tribal elders. The written version we brought, *The Code of Lekë Dukagjini*, was compiled by Shtjefën Gjeçovi, an Albanian Roman Catholic priest and ethnologist who is regarded as the father of Albanian folklore studies. His work, published four years after his death in 1933, has 1,262 articles that regulate all aspects of mountain life: economic organization of the household, hospitality, brotherhood, clan, boundaries, work, marriage, and land.

It famously codifies the principle of retributive justice, *koka për kokë*, or head for a head, in which relatives of a murder victim are obliged to seek *gjakmarje*, or blood vengeance.

Hoxha's police state effectively quashed the civic aspects of the code, but clearly its personal and social principles survived.

In times of revolt against the Ottomans, the besa was a link among different groups and tribes. And, as I often witnessed, it was a central part of the culture of post-communist Albania.

I saw it displayed in all kinds of gestures, including a lawyer literally giving me the tie off his neck after I complimented him. I should have known better, but I mentioned his shirt on one occasion. When I returned to Albania on my next trip, I found a brand new one, just like it, in my hotel room upon arrival.

On that first trip to Albania, our hosts took us on a tourist outing to the town of Krujë, about twenty miles north of Tirana.

Krujë boasts remnants of the ancient Illyrian tribe that lived there, the Albani. In 1190, it became the capital of the first Albanian state. In the early fifteenth century, it was conquered by the Ottoman Empire then recaptured in 1443 by Albania's iconic leader Skanderbeg, who successfully defended it against three Ottoman sieges.

We stopped at a mass grave in Krujë that had recently been uncovered. Up drove an entourage of shiny black cars. It was President Berisha.

Among our Albanian hosts, the reaction was reserved and hesitant. It was as if they didn't know whether to fear him or to be friendly.

It was the same reaction I saw at the Supreme Court, when I asked who wants to investigate all these guys who are not on the courts anymore.

Later that day, somebody noted the black, shiny cars never get stopped by the police.

It was a recurring theme.

THE LOST GENERATION

After a quarter of a century of rule by Eastern Europe's most brutal dictator, Enver Hoxha, Albania enjoyed a whiff of "liberalism," with the infiltration of some Western music and culture in the late 1960s and early 1970s.

My friend Fabian Kati—who fled Albania in the chaos of 1991 by clambering over the walls of the Italian embassy in Tirana with hundreds of youths—produced a film that captures this brief era and the abrupt turn in 1974.

His production, *The Hidden Documentary*,[11] tells the story of a twenty-five-minute 1972 film produced by the communist-controlled Albanian film service. It featured Albanian young people touring the country's natural and historical sites through a gauzy lens, casting the isolated Stalinist dictatorship as a bucolic dreamland.

It was meant as propaganda for foreign audiences but also to be shown in Albanian theaters to boost national pride.

But the movie was completed just as the regime launched a crackdown on "foreign influences" and "liberals,» abruptly halting the brief thaw. It was never shown to domestic audiences.

In 1972, Hoxha foreshadowed the crackdown in a speech declaring that "the ideological and cultural revolution" in Albania is "about the deep uprooting of bourgeois ideology and the strengthening of the education of the 'New Man.'"

The "New Man" concept was described by Soviet revolutionary leader Leon Trotsky in 1924 in his book "Literature and Revolution."

"Man will make it his purpose to master his own feelings, to raise his instincts to the heights of consciousness, to make them transparent, to extend the wires of his will into hidden recesses," Trotsky wrote, "and thereby to raise himself to a new plane, to create a higher social biologic type, or, if you please, a superman."

Apparently, the "superman" Hoxha had in mind—myopically devoted to spreading the socialist revolution—clashed with the image the young people portrayed in the film.

Albania's censors found the playful youth to be "too modern," Kati concludes in his documentary.

During the period of "liberalism," Albanians were allowed to install antennas capable of receiving Italian television. In the dawning of the Age of Aquarius, the entertainment programs, in particular, shocked older generations who had been virtually isolated in Hoxha's tightly controlled hermit kingdom since World War II. For Albania's youth, the foreign TV shows were a marvel that awakened a passion for more.

Hoxha pulled the plug.

Forty years later, Kati found the two producers of the state-commissioned film along with some of the students. None of them had seen the documentary they helped create.

Floriana Paskali, one of the featured students, who now describe themselves as among "the lost generation," reflected on the Albania of 1974.

"It was a terrible year. Lives were destroyed. People were scared.

They were scared of everything," she said, according to Kati's translation from Albanian.

"During that period they pulled down the antennas. They started searching houses, and people watching Italian television were deported to far-away villages. There were many frightened people paralyzed in the face of such a brutal regime.

"The whole country was overwhelmed by arrests, deportations, and forced removals," she said.

Another student featured in the film, Angelina Ceka, recalled that in the early 1970s, young people enjoyed music in the parks of Tirana and dancing in the great hall at the Drini Hotel.

"There was an orchestra and people of all different ages eating a nice dinner, dancing, having fun," she said. "But after 1974, all these things vanished. They became impossible."

Floriana Paskali noted that the documentary was made to be shown at Albanian embassies around the world "to demonstrate to foreigners how good life was in socialist Albania, on the shores of the Adriatic Sea."

But she said it "hid the truth and the most extreme fact of all—that Albania was a hell indeed."

The hell lasted another fifteen years, until a new generation of students, inspired by the revolutions that swept Eastern Europe in 1989, led a revolt against Albania's communist regime in December 1990.

Among their mentors was a law professor at Tirana's Enver Hoxha University named Zef Brozi.

Ironically—with rooftop antennas once again permissible in the relative thaw since the death of Enver Hoxha in 1985—the window to the world provided by Italian television fueled revolution.

This time, it was political rather than merely cultural, and this time the regime was on the losing side.

Albanians—perhaps far too "modern" by then for the communist regime to survive—watched in real time as Romanians, not without bloodshed, overthrew the tyrannical regime of Nicolae Ceausescu.

They did likewise, eventually, in February 1991, unleashing decades of pent-up anger in an "illegal" demonstration that filled Tirana's vast Skanderbeg Square.

As they targeted the thirty-foot-tall bronze statue of Enver Hoxha that dominated the square, police fired warning shots in the air. But there was no turning back, and when the young men toppled the symbol of tyranny, the police joined them in jubilant embraces.

In the first free elections, in March 1991, the communists, under the Party of Labor, maintained power. But after a general strike and demonstrations, the party agreed to a "stability government" that included non-communists. Amid economic collapse and social unrest, the Democratic Party won a majority in the Parliament, and party leader Sali Berisha became president.

6

EQUAL JUSTICE

ALBANIA'S DEPUTY MINISTER OF JUSTICE invited us to hold a seminar on "equal justice under the law." That phrase is nowhere in the US Constitution. But the words are inscribed on the front of the US Supreme Court building in Washington, DC. The concept comes from the Fourteenth Amendment, which says no state shall "deny to any person within its jurisdiction the equal protection of the laws."

The judges conference was to be held August 4-6, 1993.

Already, Minnesota native Kyle Tromanhauser had established a nonprofit called the Albanian Development Council that was providing resources and leadership training to the judicial system, the Ministry of Education, Parliament, and law enforcement.

Kyle and his Albanian wife, Matilda, taught a fourteen-week leadership class for justices of the Supreme Court. Many of the justices, they learned, were literally living in their offices. One lived in a 13x13-foot room with his wife, his twenty-year-old daughter, and his fifteen-year-old son. The family brought in a stove, a broken sink with a bucket underneath, and spliced together wires from other parts of the building for electricity. Other justices lived in smaller spaces on their own and traveled home on weekends by bus to visit their families.

For the seminar, we lined up a federal judge from Denver, a Philadelphia judge, and Georgia Court of Appeals Judge Dorothy Toth Beasley. The Colorado judge had to cancel because of a major case that had arisen. The Philadelphia judge was nominated to be general counsel for the US Department of Housing and Urban Development and had to attend hearings. Beasley dropped out because of a family need.

With one month to go, I didn't have any judges. And I was out of money.

That Sunday, I went to pray in our prayer room at church before the service. I felt low and wanted desperately to hear from the Lord.

Instead of a sermon that I hoped would pump me up, the choir was performing a musical production that day called "God With Us." I wanted to skip the service and go home, but Katoo urged me to stay. I'm glad I did. The first few lines of the chorus of the theme song, *Be Strong and Take Courage*, washed over me like a soothing balm:

Be strong and take courage
Do not fear or be dismayed
For the Lord will go before you
And His light will show the way
Be strong and take courage
Do not fear or be dismayed
For the one who lives within you
Will be strong in you today

After hearing those lines for about the twenty-first time, I said, "OK, Lord, I'll trust in you."

The next day, I called Lynn Buzzard of the Christian Legal Society. He said, "I have an Albanian sitting in my office right now. And I've got two judges for you."

Initially, we had four white judges lined up, but they all had to change their plans. We ended up with the perfect lineup for the theme equal justice under the law. We had a black judge from urban Philadelphia, John Braxton; a white judge from rural North Carolina, John McCormick; and a Hispanic judge from the Texas Supreme Court, Raul Gonzalez.

I couldn't have made this happen if I had tried. It turned out to be a perfect reflection of our country's diversity.

Braxton grew up in West Philadelphia. After graduating from Penn State, he served as a lieutenant in the Army and saw action in Vietnam, where he was awarded the Bronze Star with an Oak Leaf Cluster for Meritorious Service. In 1978, District Attorney Ed Rendell—later Pennsylvania governor and Democratic National Committee chairman—appointed Braxton to be the chief of the Municipal Court Unit of the Office of the District Attorney of Philadelphia. Braxton supervised a staff of seventeen and was responsible for the prosecution of more than three thousand cases annually. At the time of the seminar, he served on the Court of Common Pleas.

Gonzalez grew up in the Rio Grande Valley in Texas, where his migrant-farm-worker parents had come from Mexico. Beginning as a child, Raul worked the fields with his family, harvesting cabbage, onions, tomatoes, and cotton. In 1984, he made history when Texas Gov. Mark White appointed him as the first Hispanic justice of the state Supreme Court.

We got the judges, but we had no money, I met with my pastor, asking for financial support, and he said no. He explained that the church was behind in its giving to missionaries. I told him I certainly did not want to take anything away from the people and organizations the church already was supporting. I asked him if I could make an appeal at an adult Sunday School class, making it clear that any gift should not be given in lieu of tithing or other support.

No was his final answer.

In my car, as I prepared to drive back to my office, I hit the steering wheel in anger. It cracked. I voiced my disappointment: *Lord, you led us all this way and now we don't have the money we need to make it happen.*

Upon arrival at the office, my secretary, Linda Wood, told me a man by the name of Weyerhaeuser had called. It was Dave Weyerhaeuser, grandson of Frederick Weyerhaeuser, the founder of the iconic lumber and paper products company.

Dave, the founder of a Weyerhaeuser family trust called the Steward Foundation, told me he had heard of my work in Eastern Europe. The foundation's quarterly meeting, he said, was scheduled for the next day, and the invited speaker had to drop out at the last minute.

Could you come for an hour and tell the board what you are doing?

I canceled my appointments and drove down to Tacoma for the meeting. After my presentation, they asked me what I needed. I said a bare bones budget would be $10,000. They asked what I would need for a full budget, and I said about $15,000 to $20,000.

On the way back to Poulsbo, I made one or two stops. When I arrived at the office, a check was waiting for me. Someone, at the board's instruction, had delivered it in person.

The amount was $25,000.

In hindsight, our pastor had done us a favor, preventing us from going to our friends for help. We had to trust God.

THE GIFT OF GAVELS

Charlie Wiggins, a lawyer in nearby Bainbridge Island, Washington, helped organize the conference and planned to participate. Before we had our judges lined up, he called me and said, judges or not, we needed to give the Albanians a gift.

Wiggins served in the Army Military Intelligence Corps for four years after graduating from Princeton, rising to the rank of captain. Two years later, the governor appointed him to the Washington state Court of Appeals, and in 2011 he was elected as a justice of the Washington state Supreme Court.

We wanted to give the Albanian judges something to serve as a symbol of their authority. We discussed giving them robes, but they would cost about $400 each. How about gavels? Charlie asked how much money we had left from the donation we received from the Weyerhaeuser foundation. It was about $10,000. We called a place in Seattle that makes trophies. But with the money we had, we could buy only about forty-five or fifty.

We needed about three hundred gavels.

So, the trophy maker referred us to a gavel company in the Chicago area. We called and the manager asked how much money we had. Ten thousand dollars? For three hundred gavels?

"You're really asking a lot of me," the gavel maker said.

But between Charlie and me, we convinced him to take our $10,000 for three hundred gavels.

First, however, he had to have them made, and we needed them by August 1.

"Well, I can get them made, but can't get them shipped to you that fast," he said.

It turned out our itinerary had our connecting flight to Europe leaving from Chicago. We had an airline contact through a longtime family friend, Art's father, Art Moore Sr., who was a Delta Airlines captain. So we asked the gavel maker to deliver the gavels to Chicago O'Hare International Airport, and we would take it from there.

He said, "You can't do that. That won't work."

Trust us, we said, we'll take care of it.

The gavel maker agreed to send them to the airport to meet our flight. Art Sr. made an annotation on our tickets indicating we were going to add baggage in Chicago.

We got to the counter in Chicago for our Swiss Air flight to Zurich. The stern agent clearly wasn't happy with us.

"You are breaking all the rules, Mr. Sherrard. I can't say it strongly enough. You are not supposed to do this," she said.

We told her the story of the Albanian judges, explaining that many were forced to live in their offices, and they lacked basic supplies, like paper.

I urged her to open a box or two.

There they were, individually wrapped.

We were not charged for any excess baggage.

ACROSS CULTURE AND LANGUAGE

Charlie and I went from Zurich to Rome, where we met Judge Braxton from Philadelphia and Judge McCormick from North Carolina to plan our sessions.

With three judges and four lawyers from around the United States, we needed to communicate—across culture and language barriers, no less—a completely different way of understanding law. They had no comprehension of an independent judiciary.

We decided to do a mock trial to illustrate equal justice under the law. Then we would emphasize the lessons from the trial in our speeches.

Before the seminar, our hosts treated us once again to a side trip, taking us to the ancient city of Berat. On the way, we stopped on the coast of the Adriatic Sea, just south of the port city of Durres.

Concrete bunkers littered the beach and the fields across the road. In the Hoxha era, they served as a visible symbol of the regime's narrative that the imperialist West, led by the United States, or neighboring Yugoslavia or Greece were poised at any moment to invade their socialist paradise.

In fact, under Hoxha's "bunkerization," more than 170,000 bunkers had been built throughout the country by 1983, an average of nearly fifteen every square mile. [12]

The strategy, we were told, based on their studies of the Normandy D-Day landing, was to give up the bunkers on the coast. They planned to position their defense back at a second or third tier. Hoxha had in mind a civilian, guerrilla-style war similar to the Albanian resistance he led during World War II.

In Berat, which traces its back to the sixth century B.C. as a settlement, we had a wonderful time getting to know the people and enjoying their remarkable hospitality. We stayed with a man who once was an official artist for the Communist Party. They sang some of their traditional songs in their beautiful, haunting polyphonic tones. They wanted us to sing, too. The only song we all knew was *Take Me Out to the Ball Game*. It wasn't exactly choir quality, but the Albanians loved it.

The next morning in Tirana, we arrived early at the conference room. But the janitors on duty there refused to open the door. It was one day before the conference was to begin, and the director demanded a bribe of $3,000 in cash to let us in.

We prayed Deuteronomy 31:6: "Be strong and courageous, do not fear or be afraid." The next day the janitors opened the door for us.

At the seminar, the mock trial was a hit. John Braxton, with his deep, resonant voice, narrated. When he thought it appropriate, he interrupted to explain what was happening.

Charlie Wiggins was the prosecutor, and I was the defense attorney. We presented all the phases of a trial.

I was joined on the trip by author Frank Peretti. I had helped him with some of the legal elements in his blockbuster fiction book *Piercing the Darkness*, and he was intrigued by my stories about the new Albania. Frank was particularly interested in the spiritual dynamics of a country in which religion had been completely banned.

Frank had a role in the mock trial. He had stolen a bicycle from the mayor's porch and got caught. Police officers beat a confession out of him with a rubber hose.

The principle was that beating a confession out of someone does not necessarily produce reliable testimony and in our system is not admissible in court. We also covered Miranda rights and the right to legal counsel.

Our advice was that Albania should consider protecting these rights in their new constitution.

We split into six breakout groups, each with an American and an interpreter. Kyle and Matilda Tromanhauser had developed a team of college-age young people proficient in English who were key to the success of the seminars, accurately communicating the principles in a winsome way. Katoo and I became close to some of the Albanian interpreters, including one who ended up attending Seattle Pacific University.

Charlie said that, for him, the greatest reward was to "see the light come on in the eyes of the judges when they saw a principle of constitutional law and what it meant."

Jay Brown, who had just completed his first year of law school at Syracuse, played the policeman who arrested Frank. Jay had just learned that he had been accepted as a member of the law review. I told the minister of justice, and they had a special ceremony for him.

That was my first introduction to besa. They understood what it meant to this young man.

Sam did a study of the Golden Rule. I believe the Golden Rule of "do unto others as you would have them do unto you" is the ultimate statement of due process of law. Nearly every religion has a version of the Golden Rule.

The conflict in any nation usually comes in the overlap of the three institutions of society: church, state, and family. The key is to have an independent judiciary that can't be controlled by the legislature or the executive.

That's what we were trying to get across in Bulgaria.

It's a simple message but not one that is easily adopted. We were often transported in cars with government license plates, and on one occasion we were with the speaker of Parliament's general counsel, Perikli Zaharia, riding from our hotel to the Supreme Court. The driver took a shortcut, barreling down a one-way street in the wrong direction.

A policeman directing traffic began blowing his whistle madly.

Peri leaned out the window and pointed to the license plate from the Supreme Court. He shouted to the officer, perhaps with tongue only slightly in cheek, "The rule of law!"

BASIC NEEDS

The Supreme Court's chief justice, Nuro Hot, and his colleagues regarded the first seminar, in 1993, as a success and looked forward to another in 1994.

But it became clear that our collaboration needed to go beyond education. Zef was elected chief justice September 23, 1993. And in a letter to me that December, he emphasized that educating judges needed to be accompanied by helping them meet basic needs. And he meant basic.

"We have no library, no system of annotation for our laws, nor do we even have a common location where all of our laws are kept for the benefit of our judges," Zef wrote. "In almost all of the courts, we do not even have typewriters or photocopy machines."

The courts, including the highest, also lacked a reporting system.

"We have very little basis for understanding and developing a code of ethics for our judges, and we have many problems in determining what our judicial standards should be, since our background in ethics is only from our old system."

Zef concluded by thanking us for the fax machine we had given them. But he noted that among thirty-six judicial districts, six appellate courts, the Constitutional Court, and the Supreme Court, it was the only one they had.

THE DICTATOR'S HIDEAWAY

Judges Braxton and Gonzalez joined us again for the July 1994 seminar, and this time we had Georgia Court of Appeals Judge Dorothy Beasley and Washington state Supreme Court Judge Robert Utter.

Before the seminar began, Zef and some of his judicial colleagues hosted my wife, Katoo, and me, and our entourage of American judges at a villa in the city of Vlore on the spectacular Adriatic coast.

It was a hot and extremely bumpy ride in our small bus, with the driver frequently slamming on the brakes to avoid hitting a horse-drawn cart, a pedestrian, or a chicken in the road.

At one point during the journey, we felt a sudden sprinkle of water hit us from behind. The culprit was Judge Beasley, armed with a squirt gun.

It was the Fourth of July, and the Georgia judge also had packed American flags and sparklers in her luggage in anticipation of a celebration.

That night, we stayed in a villa in Vlore overlooking the Adriatic Sea.

"Now I know we are free," Zef told us at dinner time.

After dinner, Katoo asked him what he meant by that statement.

"We're in the dictator's villa," he replied, "and if you even mentioned the word 'America,' you would be sent to prison."

"Not only are we here in this place that was reserved only for the communist elite, but we are also here with Americans."

On the veranda, as the sun set, the Albanians waved the tiny stars and stripes, and the sparklers with their new American friends.

We sang *The Star-Spangled Banner*, with visions of Hoxha rolling over in his grave.

It wasn't until at least ten years later that our hosts had the courage to inform Katoo and me that we had slept that night in the bedroom that was reserved for Enver Hoxha himself.

THE MIRACLE OF THE ROBES

When Charlie and I discussed possible gifts for the judges attending the 1993 seminar, robes were out of the question, because they would cost as much as $400 a piece. Supplying the gavels was a miracle in itself.

But for some reason, Zef was promising that any judges attending the 1994 conference would receive a judicial robe.

He didn't tell me that, and it was about a month before we were to depart for Tirana that I found out.

Charlie called and told me he had secured thirty choir robes at his mothers' Presbyterian church in Dothan, Alabama. I figured that if the Presbyterians could come up with them, the Lutherans of Norwegian Poulsbo and environs could, too. In short order, we had two hundred black robes.

It turned out that most church choirs had abandoned black robes. But many had them in their storage, apparently thinking they might come back in style someday.

When we arrived in Albania, we discovered we were ninety-two robes short. We decided with Zef that those who came the farthest should receive them, and the judges from Tirana and nearby Durres could get theirs on the next visit.

Utter and Brozi led off the conference July 7, 1994, with an address titled "The Importance of an Independent Judiciary," followed by a panel discussion and an address by Dorothy Beasley called "Judicial Impartiality."

The event was held in the Pyramid of Tirana, a glass building modeled after the famous tombs reserved for Egyptian pharaohs. Completed in 1988 as the Enver Hoxha Museum, it facetiously was known by the populace as the "Enver Hoxha Mausoleum."

We did another mock trial, this time a boundary line dispute between neighbors. Katoo was one neighbor, and Betty Utter, the wife of Washington state Supreme Court Justice Bob Utter, the other. Betty beat me over the head with her umbrella, and Bob found her in contempt of court and put her in jail.

Everybody got a big kick out of that. We gave Betty the annual "Skanderbeg Best Actress Award" at the concluding dinner.

We were trying to present ideas from our judicial system. At the same time, we wanted to be respectful of their own traditions and background. We were careful not to come on too strongly.

Once a day, somebody was assigned to say, in his own words, that although we've been at it in the US for more than two hundred years, we still don't have it completely right. We'll do our best to tell you about our system, the good and the bad. Your job is to choose what will work best for your country, because you know it better than we do.

It occurred to me at the time that we were witnessing the birth of a new nation.

I felt like I was in a time machine going back to Philadelphia in 1787 when the Continental Congress assembled and wrote the US Constitution. There was the back and forth, the balancing of interests, the arguments, the debate, and compromise. But this was right in front of my eyes, not a civics textbook.

We discussed the selection and removal of judges, pointing out that the power to remove judges amounts to a veto over the courts. That's why, we explained, federal judges in the United States have a life tenure. States require an impeachment proceeding to remove a judge.

A GIFT FROM GOD

On the day we were to distribute the robes, Katoo and I had planned lunch with Cynthia Caples, the public information officer at the US Embassy in Tirana. We wanted to treat her to a meal to thank her for producing the conference books. She had translated the agenda and all of the judge's briefs into Albanian, with an English translation on one side of each page.

We went to her office to pick her up, and an aide arrived, informing her that there was a package that had arrived for her at the airport. Time was of the essence, because typically at that time if diplomatic packages weren't collected right away, they would go to customs and might not be seen again.

Cynthia apologized for canceling lunch, excused herself and went with the aide to the airport.

I went to the afternoon session at the pyramid building, where they had resumed the mock trial.

As the session was winding down, I looked up and saw Cynthia in the back of the room, trying to get my attention. She was making a time-out symbol with her hands.

I went back to meet her and find out what she wanted. It was about the package she had picked up at the airport. It had robes in it. Ninety-two robes. Exactly.

The shipping information had been torn off, and we, to this day, don't know where the robes came from. And we have no idea why they were sent to Cynthia, since she had no known association with me or the seminar organizers.

Matilda Tromanhauser recruited a group of Albanian women to iron the robes. At the end of the seminar, all 292—one for each of the 292 judges in attendance—were neatly laid out by size. In a receiving line, we had people assisting each judge with donning a new robe.

7

RESISTANCE

WHEN ENVER HOXHA SEIZED POWER IN 1944, there were about 180 Roman Catholic clergy members in Albania. But within just four years, more than half were killed by the regime, some through systematic torture. Hoxha accused priests of collaborating with the Italian and Nazi fascists, and many were framed as enemies of the state by hiding ammunition in their living quarters.

Among them was Father Zef Pllumi of the northern city of Shkodra.

A family from Mirdita with whom I often stayed, aptly named the Mirditas, introduced me to the Franciscan priest, who spent a total of twenty-six years in prison. At age twenty-two, Father Zef was arrested by the secret police, the Sigurimi, for the first time and charged with possession of arms and plotting an insurrection.

The Sigurimi turned the seminary where he resided into a prison. The dining room, he told me, became a torture chamber for hundreds of believers and priests. Screams were heard day and night, he said.

One of the most common practices was to tie the prisoner with a rope under his armpits and then suspend him from a tree or a stair railing for days, with his toes partially touching the floor.[13] After the priests were untied, they were taken to the investigation room for interrogation, where they would endure hour-long beatings with batons and iron bars. Their bodies would become so bloodied that many were unrecognizable. After the beatings, there was electric shock treatment. The regime's sanctioned tormentors attached live wires behind both ears and used the handle of an old-fashioned telephone to generate a current. The priest said that as soon as the Sigurimi believed a prisoner's spirit had been broken, a document with criminal charges was placed in front of him, and he was told to sign. But Father Zef never broke and was released after three years of sadistic torture and interrogation.

In 1951, Hoxha initiated a second phase of repression by shutting down seminaries and banning religious instruction to youth. Hoxha's persecution was so extreme that even Stalin cautioned him against being so aggressive. That same year, the Albanian dictator ordered the execution by firing squad of twenty-two intellectuals without trial on false charges of high treason.[14]

The Sigurimi listened to all the sermons to ensure they adhered to the party line. But the intimidation and threats only drew more people to church, and many buildings destroyed during the first stage of persecution were rebuilt by the faithful.

In 1967, Hoxha reacted. Embracing the Cultural Revolution in China, he went further than Mao, Stalin, or any other dictator in the twentieth century by declaring his nation to be the world's first atheist state.[15]

There were to be no state-controlled religious organizations, as existed in the Soviet Union and in the Eastern bloc nations under Moscow's hegemony. Hoxha declared that any symbol of religious belief or worship must be eliminated as he dispatched teams of party activists throughout the country.

By the end of the year, any house of worship that had not been turned into a cinema, sports hall, warehouse, or other non-religious facility had been destroyed—more than two thousand in all.

Already, Albania had broken off relations with the Soviet Union, which Hoxha believed had betrayed the Marxist-Leninist revolution since the death of Stalin. Khrushchev's condemnation of the cult of personality and his theory of peaceful coexistence in foreign relations angered Hoxha. Albania's Institute of Marxist-Leninist Studies, led by Hoxha's wife, Nexhmije, cited Vladimir Lenin himself to justify its hardline expansionist stance: "The fundamental principle of the foreign policy of a socialist country and of a Communist party is proletarian internationalism; not peaceful coexistence."[16]

In direct violation of the 1946 Albanian constitution's protections of freedom of conscience and religious practice, the party revoked the charters of the Orthodox, Roman Catholic, and Muslim communities.

Hoxha deployed what he called the "sharp knife of the party" against religion, which he saw as an organized political threat to the regime as well as a "poison" in the hearts of the people. He launched his war on "religious ideology" with a February 6, 1967, speech followed by a guidance letter from the central committee of the Party of Labor.

"Religion is the opium of the people. We must do our best to make everybody understand this, even those who have been poisoned (who are not few in numbers)," he wrote. "We must cure them. This is neither an easy job, nor impossible."[17]

That year, he also laid out his case for religion as a political threat.

"Islam has been the ideology of the Turkish occupier," he said. "The Orthodox religion has been the ideology of the Greek chauvinists who have occupied the country in the past, and Catholics—with the Vatican at the center—has been the ideology of the Italian invaders, Austrian imperialism, and Italian fascism."

Religious beliefs were completely banned in the constitution of the People's Republic of Albania in 1976, nine years after Hoxha's speech.

Article 37 of the constitution declared: "The state recognizes no religion and supports and develops atheistic propaganda to engage people in the materialistic scientific worldview." Article 55, meanwhile, prohibited the establishment of any organization of a religious character.

OVERCOME EVIL WITH GOOD

In 1967, Father Zef was arrested again. He eventually was convicted on the manufactured charge of preparing to flee the country to protest church closures to the United Nations. He was sentenced to twenty-five years imprisonment with hard labor, and the torture resumed.

Father Zef told me there were offers to make him a permanent minister of culture if he would renounce his faith.

He said the guards would joke that there were so many evil spirits out to get him, they fought against each other, and in so doing spared his life.

Toward the end of our meeting, I asked this man who had endured unspeakable suffering about his view of good and evil. He recalled a guard who had been especially brutal to him.

Prisoners were forced to tar the roofs of apartment buildings every summer. The guards would block off access to staircases and have prisoners climb a ladder to the roof.

One day, Father Zef was waiting to be retrieved. The guard who had tormented him was climbing the ladder when it broke away from the building and began falling to the side.

The priest had to make a split-second decision.

He reached over and stabilized the ladder. The guard never beat him again.

I almost felt as if I had been in the presence of Christ when I was with him. As we departed, I said, "You remind me of what Christ said about Peter: 'On this rock I will build my church.'"

"Overcoming evil with good" was on my mind as I dined one evening in May 1995 in Tirana with Thimio Kondi, a native of the southern Albanian city of Gjirokaster. I first got to know Thimio when he was serving on the Supreme Court and he accompanied us to Hoxha's villa in Vlore on the coast in 1994. Now, exasperated by corruption, he had just resigned from Albania's Constitutional Court.

I couldn't possibly know what it was like to be in his position, but I suggested at one point that "when good men do nothing, evil prevails."

I didn't think he could object to that age-old axiom.

"You don't understand," he replied, "under the old regime, they used to lop off your head. Now, they have your wife lose her job or they fail your son in school. They tell the neighbors the garbage isn't being picked up on your block because you're a member of the Mafia."

CRACKDOWN

The next day we went to the office the Parliament had set aside for us at the Supreme Court. Petrit Plloci, now a Supreme Court justice, walked in with a long look on his face.

"Petrit, what's the matter?" I asked.

"I heard on the 11 o'clock news that Parliament is going to vote to remove me tomorrow, along with Tefta Zaka and Vitore Tusha," he said.

"It can't be stopped, because Berisha is behind it."

Parliament members, who are tasked with electing the members of the high court, charged that the three justices did not meet the qualifications spelled out in the new law. They alleged the justices wrongly counted their time serving as assistant judges to satisfy the constitutional requirement that they must serve for seven years as a judge to qualify for the Supreme Court.

"Petrit, they can't do that," I said. "The Parliament already has vetted their qualifications. You just need to mount your defense."

It became clear that the real reason the three were targeted was that they were allies of Chief Justice Zef Brozi, who had signed off on several opinions that went against the government.[18]

Further, according to the April 1991 law that established the court system, a Supreme Court justice can be removed from office "only on the basis of a reasoned decision of the People's Assembly when proven that he or she has committed a serious criminal act, specifically provided for by law, or when he or she is mentally disabled."

I had a prior appointment scheduled that afternoon with Kazara Koti, the head of the Albanian Human Rights Documentation Center, to talk about human rights issues.

I told her what was happening in Parliament the next day.

"That isn't right. The intent of Parliament had been to include service as an assistant judge,» she said.

Kazara immediately changed the agenda for our meeting.

"We're going to talk about saving the Supreme Court," she said. «I have to get my attorney.»

In walked her attorney, who was none other than Thimio, fresh from our conversation the night before about the cost of confronting evil.

Kazara asked Thimio if he would be willing to stand up for the judges.

He said he needed to get permission from his wife, Alexandria, because of the cost to the family. She said yes.

We developed a lobbying strategy to visit eighteen Parliament members at various restaurants in town. We drafted a letter that we gave to each deputy about the importance of an independent judiciary.

We showed the lawmakers that what the Parliament was doing was illegal.

"We're going to beat them," Kazara said.

In addition, Kazara set up an appointment for Petrit, Thimio, and me to meet with the chief of Albania's largest newspaper, Koha Jonë, which translates into English as "our time."

GIVE US A SIGN

We arrived at the paper's office at 5 p.m. But Petrit and Thimio told me they didn't want to go inside.

"This guy is all for the Democratic Party, all for Berisha. He doesn't like judges," Petrit explained. "He thinks we're too independent. We don't have a prayer with this guy."

I said, "Well, prayer is something we need. You know I'm a

Christian. You've been to our home."

So they agreed to pray.

I just said, "Lord, if we're on the right path, give us a sign. If we're on the wrong path, give us a sign. Show us how we should be responding to this."

They decided they would join me after all.

We introduced ourselves to the burley editor, and he sat down in front of his desk.

"I have assigned Martin Leka to write an opinion for the newspaper on this case," the editor said. "He can come and take pictures if he wants and report on what's happening in Parliament tomorrow.

Martin came to meet us.

"Mr. Sherrard?" he said. "Weren't you in Albania last summer?"

"Yes, I was," I replied.

"Did you give some advice to a translator that was working with you? Her mother worked for a newspaper. And it was about a reporter who was in jail?"

"Yes, I did."

"I've been looking for you, because I owe you," he said. "Your advice got me out of jail."

Petrit's and Thimio's eyes grew wide.

Leka, along with Aleksander Frangaj, editor-in-chief of Koha Jonë, were arrested in January 1994 on trumped up charges of revealing state secrets and slander.[19] A month later, Leka was found guilty, but Frangaj was acquitted.

Leka had reported the publication of a Ministry of Defense order, signed by Minister of Defense Safet Zhulali, that ordered Albanian Army officers to leave their weapons in the barracks when off duty. Koha Jonë reprinted a copy of the order and ran an accompanying text written by Leka titled "The Disarming of the Military." Leka was charged with slander against the minister. Frangaj, as the responsible editor, was charged with revealing state secrets. Both were imprisoned.

The arrests were the fifth against Koha Jonë journalists in the previous two years and the second against Frangaj.

Leka interviewed Petrit and reported the story. He quoted Petrit saying, "I know the Parliament will do the right thing tomorrow."

THE WHOLE WORLD IS WATCHING

Meanwhile, Zef had just returned from a meeting with the Council of Europe in Strasbourg, France. He drafted an open letter to Parliament that began with, "We are at a critical crossroads for Albania."

"In the past four years, Parliament has made many courageous decisions to establish and protect our new democracy," the letter said.

And now, "Europe and the whole world are watching to see how we will proceed."

Zef told the deputies he heard about the proposal to remove the judges in Strasbourg, and the news "was devastating to our friends in Europe." Many, he said, now question Albania's commitment to freedom and democracy.

He reminded the lawmakers that international standards require that judges be independent, and other branches of government must not exert direct control over the judiciary.

But several recent events, he said, "raise serious questions about the future of an independent judiciary in Albania."

One was the unsuccessful attempt to remove him as chief justice, and others included moves to give the Ministry of Justice sole authority to hire and dismiss judicial employees as well as control over the judicial budget.

"How can the judiciary be independent if another branch of government controls its staff and budget?" he asked.

Zef pointed out that he was a member of Parliament when the law on judges was drafted. He argued that it was the clear intent of the members to count other judicial experience as part of the required seven years.

"It has been said that injustice triumphs when good people do nothing," he wrote. "Parliament has many good people with the courage to act so that justice will win. I am confident that the trust of those who desire a free and just society will not be broken."

In conclusion he said, "Today we have a chance to tell the people of Albania, our friends in Europe and the entire world that Albanian will be free and that we have a judicial system which will guarantee our rights and freedoms for generations to come."

The letter was sent to all Western embassies and hand-delivered to every member of Parliament.

'TICKETS TO MY OWN HANGING'

Petrit informed me that the Parliament would not let him in the gallery to observe the vote.

"They're deciding whether to remove you, and they won't let you in?"

"No. I can't get in. I tried to get tickets."

"Only God can save this thing," Petrit said.

"Well, let's pray," I said.

So, we prayed.

I had a meeting the next morning with the speaker of Parliament, Peter Arbnori, that had been previously scheduled. Dorothy Beasley, the Georgia judge, had a letter from former President Jimmy Carter expressing willingness to work with Albania to form a judiciary committee that would independently establish the court's budget. Berisha and his Democratic Party had been using their power over the budget as a lever.

I was to present the letter from Carter to the speaker of Parliament. I had an appointment at 10:30 a.m. The Parliament session was to begin at 11.

While waiting at Arbnori's office, we watched as all of the Parliament members we had seen the day before walked by us to meet with the speaker.

Finally, the speaker's assistant said, "Mr. Sherrard, we're really sorry, but you're not going to be able to see him."

But she went on, "I know this involves the former US president. So, here are four tickets to the gallery. You can take anybody you want to go to the gallery with you."

Petrit and Thimio were speechless.

"I don't know how you do it," Petrit eventually said. "I tried to get tickets to go to my own hanging and couldn't get them."

Petrit joined us in the gallery. The deputies that we had talked to the day before saw us up there and gave us two thumbs up.

As we looked on, Parliament scratched the removal of the justices from the agenda. Petrit, Tefta, and Vitore finished their terms on the Supreme Court.

Later, I was informed that it was our presence in the gallery that prompted the move.

Before leaving Albania, I had lunch with Carl Siebentritt, the US Embassy's political section officer. In our conversation, I realized that Parliament could put the removal of the judges back on the agenda any time they wanted. We hadn't closed the deal.

"You need to get somebody who carries weight," he said.

Bob Utter, the chief justice of the Washington State Supreme Court, was the man for the job.

At the airport, I called his home number from an Albanian cell-phone. His wife, Betty, answered.

Betty would always give me a hard time about taking Bob away from her and the family. She had just retired from Saint Martin's College in Olympia, Washington, where she was an adjunct teacher in the evenings. Her day job was intervention specialist—a school counselor—helping kids in trouble.

Her skills and experience were of great value when she and Bob helped mediate a reconciliation for judges in Rwanda.

This time, if Bob were to answer the call, it would mean missing her retirement party.

I told Bob, "You need to go tomorrow and close this deal, because I'm a lawyer from Poulsbo, and I don't have any clout.»

Bob dropped everything and was on a plane to Tirana the next day.

He closed the deal.

SABOTAGE

We worked with Zef to co-sponsor the third Albanian Judicial Conference July 24-28, 1995, in Vlore and Tirana with the theme "The Importance of an Independent Judiciary."

During the conference, Albanians had a glimpse of American justice on their TV screens via the O.J. Simpson trial. It was carried by CNN International, which was available in Europe via a paid subscription to a satellite TV package.

But any Albanian with a rabbit-ear antenna could watch CNN and other channels, thanks to the giant satellite dish and transmitter on nearby Mt. Dajti that illegally beamed the signal across the capital city for free.

The minister of justice, Hektor Frasheri, threatened that if any justices went to the seminar, they would lose their pay for the month. Nevertheless, 150 judges showed up and many of the prosecutors as well.

Petrit Plloci, who then was the president of the Association of Judges of Albania, was quoted in the English-language Albanian Daily News[20] saying Frasheri's threat was "another attempt by the minister of justice to hold under his dependence courts and judges." Petrit urged judges to attend and "not let their independence be sold."

Zef told the Daily News the move was a "continuation of attempts by the minister of justice to dictate to judges and courts and restore political and exclusive authority over juridical power."

He said Frasheri was attempting to "sabotage" the event "because he is afraid" of the judges banding together with one voice. The judges, Zef said, are "becoming ever more conscious that they cannot and should not accept orders and dictates by" political officials regarding the activities of their association.

Zef maintained that resolute stance in his speech to kick off the third annual conference. He began with the charge that the "independence of the courts and the judges had been violated and endangered."

"Some segments of the political and executive power, through unethical and intriguing ways and means, have opposed the attempts to create any independent judicial power in Albania," he said.

Zef then made it more personal.

"These shortsighted politicians, who step on the pure ideals of the December 1990 movement, try to do their best to have courts and judges as obedient tools to accomplish their dishonest goals," he charged.

"Such hypocritical politicians," he continued, "put chains" on judges who abide by the "sanctity of the law" and equal justice.

Zef said the Supreme Court, through some of its recent decisions, had been "winning the hope and trust of the people" that their rights would be protected.

But that trust was being eroded by judges who had "become subservient and tools" of politicians, he said, warning their "reward will be contempt." He condemned "some segments of political and executive power" who are trying to divide and "shut the mouth" of the judges and the Judges Association.

Zef, making his rebuke even more personal, quoted the revered early twentieth century Albanian writer, statesman, and founder of the Orthodox Church of Albania, Fan Noli.

"As Noli used to say, 'They have a devilish spirit and all the necessary means to accomplish their evil goals,'" Zef said, referring to Albania's current leaders.

"Judges are being enticed with trips abroad, higher positions and jobs for their relatives," he said.

"And when they see that such ways do not work, they use threatening, insult, slander," demotion, surveillance by the secret police and "an unscrupulous campaign through the press and T.V.," Zef said.

"Unfortunately, the Albanian judges are afraid. They do not feel they are secure and untouchable as judges."

He took aim at the minister of justice, who he said will be "known in history as the minister of all injustices."

He chastised the Judges Association for remaining "dumb, deaf, and indifferent toward the attacks the judiciary is facing," particularly the attempt to remove the association's president, Petrit, along with Zaka and Tusha, from the Supreme Court.

After his speech, Zef thought judges around the world would support him. But it was the beginning of the end for him.

PERSONAL DIFFERENCES

In July, Zef asked me to be the best man in his wedding at the city's largest Roman Catholic church, which had been turned into a cinema during the Hoxha era.

At his wedding reception at a restaurant, I had a discussion with the ranking member of Parliament, who told me the judges were too strong and needed to be reined in.

"What do you mean by that?" I asked him.

"Well, we haven't decided how we're going to do it, but we've got to show that the executive is in control," he replied.

The discussion took place not long after the Supreme Court ruled against President Berisha's wishes in a case in which I gave counsel regarding an Albanian extradited from Greece.

On September 12, 1995, Berisha met President Bill Clinton in the White House. Berisha offered NATO the further use of Albanian ports and airfields, and an agreement on military cooperation with the US was signed one month later in Washington.

In the talking points crafted by Warren Christopher, the secretary of state, Clinton was advised to press Berisha on the "independence of the judiciary."[21]

"Some observers claim that personal differences have intruded into the wordings of the courts," Christopher wrote. "Judges must not have to consider that they could lose their positions as a result of carrying out their duties."

In a joint US-Albania press release, the two nations declared their intention to develop an independent judiciary in the Balkan state.

But immediately after Berisha arrived back in Tirana, a series of events began to unfold that belied his assurance.

8

PROTEST

AT A DINNER AFTER THE JUDICIAL CONFERENCE IN JULY, a Parliament member disclosed to me that President Berisha, after returning from the White House, was planning to remove Zef as chief justice.

The deputy told me that upon his return, Berisha would create the impression that he had the tacit approval of President Clinton to remove the chief justice of Albania's highest court.

The deputy noted it was the same tactic used by former dictator Enver Hoxha following visits to Moscow.

Zef and Berisha previously had been close personal friends. In fact, it was Berisha, in September 1993, who appointed Zef as chief justice of the Supreme Court. Zef had been elected to Parliament the previous year as Democratic Party representative for Mirdita, where he was born. And he had become chairman of the Parliament's Law Commission.

From 1982 to 1992, Zef was on the faculty of law of the University of Tirana. He assisted in the 1990s in the birth of the student movement, which led to the collapse of the communist regime. He was elected, along with other professors and students, to present the movement's demands and negotiate with the last communist dictator, the successor to Hoxha, Ramiz Alia.

WHAT WE WANTED TO HEAR

In our early meetings, Berisha was very convincing, assuring my colleagues and me of his support for an independent judiciary.

We were so impressed with Berisha's grasp of the facts and principles that we were willing to overlook the proposed constitutional provisions for a strong presidency. Berisha's command of English, affable demeanor, and willingness to articulate important democratic principles made him persuasive. He said what we wanted to hear.

But my first concern about Berisha came when Zef posed a question to Justice Sandra Day O'Connor on the visit of Albanian justices I arranged to the US Supreme Court. Zef asked O'Connor what she would do if the president called and suggested how a case should be decided.

In later conversations, Zef disclosed that although they had been close friends, President Berisha had refused to communicate since Zef freed two imprisoned journalists in 1994 against the will of the government.

Early in 1995, the Democratic Party brought a vote to Parliament to remove Zef's judicial immunity. After intense debate, and a preliminary vote to have a secret ballot, the measure was defeated.

But other attacks on the judiciary followed. Berisha got his way through an authority established in April 1992 called the High Council of Justice, which was headed by Berisha himself. Through the council, which existed until 2017, Berisha was able to summarily remove and replace many lower court judges without a hearing or constitutionally required due process.

According to Zef, many judges were appointed not for their legal qualifications but for their loyalty to the ruling Democratic Party. One judge, Alfred Vasili, was appointed even though he didn't have a law degree.

In a typical meeting of the High Council of Justice, Zef said, the minister of justice would propose several candidates for appointments as judges. A vote would then be taken without any discussion about the candidates' legal credentials and qualifications.

The Democratic Party held the executive and legislative branches, and it also had the judiciary in its grip by controlling the budgets. The party insisted that the minister of justice had the right to appoint staff in the courts. That included selecting even the personal secretary of the chief justice.

WE'RE SURROUNDED

On September 6, 1995, Zef telephoned me.

"The court is completely surrounded by police," he said. "Two members of the court were roughed up just trying to get into the building."

He said staff members were being detained or denied access. One of the barred staff members was the director of administration, who supervised, among other things, all the docketing of the court.

But the government was denying publicly that it was placing any pressure on the court, insisting the police were there only to protect the judges. Many credible sources told us the government's response was laughable, because they had seen the bolstered police presence and the abusive tactics with their own eyes.

Just two weeks later, on September 21, 1995, I was at my office in Poulsbo when I received an urgent call from Zef.

"The Parliament just removed me from office," he said.

Zef told me he had been blindsided, learning of the move only after the vote had taken place. The unusual evening vote had been scheduled when every party, except for the ruling Democratic Party, was holding their convention.

According to the constitution, there are only two causes for removal of a justice: commission of a serious crime or mental incompetence. And neither claim was made.

During my call with Zef, we heard the telltale clicking of a wiretap and a loud beep that apparently indicated the tape had run out.

"Whoever is listening, I'll count to ten so you can adjust your interceptor," Zef said. "One, two, three. … Did you get it tuned?"

I made immediate plans to head to Tirana.

INVESTIGATION

One of my law partners in Poulsbo, John Johnson, moved with his family to Tirana for eight months, from January to August in 1995. They rented the upper level of the home of the Mirditas, the family Katoo and I stayed with on our first visits.

During that time, John had a key role in strengthening relationships and developing new ones. Among many things, he distributed office equipment and paper supplies obtained through the generosity of the Washington State Bar Association and other state bar associations.

John had now moved back to Poulsbo, and he joined me on a trip to Tirana to come to Zef's aid, arriving at Rinas Airport on the afternoon of October 4.

We were met by our driver and translator, who reported that the situation was tense. To avoid compromising any members of the court, we made only indirect contact. We learned from an insider that members of the court were under constant surveillance. And Avni Shehu, Zef Brozi's replacement, was not taking any action without the consent of the minister of justice or Berisha.

We had decided before our arrival that we would conduct our investigation as openly as possible. We were followed the entire time we were in Albania. At the airport, our luggage was searched, and letters were torn open.

We met with many members of Parliament from several parties, most of the members of the Supreme Court, the Albanian Helsinki Committee, US Embassy officials, the president of Amnesty International in Albania, and other Western observers and knowledgeable Albanians.

We had dinner with Zef and Diana at the Tirana International Hotel on our first night.

"You're never going to be able to break this one, Sherrard," Zef said.

Before answering, I recalled that back in June—during Berisha's attempt to remove the three justices—John's 5-year-old daughter, Meredith, asked John and I, "Have you prayed yet?"

"You're right," I replied to Zef. "But God can."

It was clear that we were being watched. When the waiters approached our table, the Brozis reminded us to be careful of our conversation. The couple constantly scanned the area, looking for hidden microphones.

Zef and Diana acknowledged they were concerned for their personal safety. They said that when they traveled to Zef's hometown of Mirdita in the north after his removal, they were followed by three cars, which continued tailing them during the week that they were there.

Zef believed that his removal was contrary to the law, but under the political circumstances there was little he could do about it. Berisha controlled the judges' paychecks. Ultimately, Zef's only ally turned out to be the media.

In some ways, Zef was relieved that the battle was over and the pressure off. But he was extremely disappointed with the outcome and the harm his removal would bring to the cause of judicial independence.

FATAL ERRORS

On our first night in Tirana, a Socialist Party member of Parliament, Pandeli Majko, went the entire night without sleep to write a memo to me in English regarding the errors that Parliament members made in their removal of Zef.

He brought the document to us at breakfast.

"Handle this with care," he said. "I'm taking a lot of risks here."

For one, the Parliament didn't give proper notice of the vote. Any notice for an emergency meeting on a subject that had not been brought up before Parliament must be made at least thirty days in advance. They didn't do that by a long shot.

There were six standalone fatal errors in the procedure. The biggest was the lack of a quorum. So, we zeroed in on that. Who are they counting as a yes vote who was not even present? I went to the parliamentary secretaries and got sworn statements translated by an official translator into English and French. The readout of the vote, signed by two secretaries, proved that they didn't have a quorum.

We also had a statement of one of the lawmakers who was not present but was recorded as having voted. Three other members reported to the press that they also were listed in the vote count without being present.

After meetings with several deputies of Parliament who fervently briefed us on the illegitimate vote, we met with a member of the Democratic Party, Mr. Puto. He gave us, literally, the "party line."

What was the serious criminal offense Zef Brozi was charged with? Puto claimed that Zef had politicized his office as chief justice of the Supreme Court. Later in the conversation, I asked Puto if he thought Zef would be charged with a crime. He admitted Zef hadn't done anything that warranted a penal charge.

Nevertheless, Puto staunchly defended the actions of Parliament. But his answers were often so outrageous—we had the proof in printouts of the vote—that another Parliament member who was at the meeting couldn't contain himself and frequently broke out in laughter.

I met again with Zef and reviewed the documents we had obtained from Parliament. He was visibly moved by the evidence of numerous improprieties.

But at the same time, Zef feared having the evidence in hand and asked that it be handled discreetly. He had been told he would not be charged and had been given assurances of his personal safety.

But Zef believed that security would continue only as long as he remained passive and didn't fight back.

WE CAN'T INTERFERE

I went to the US Embassy in Tirana and met with the chargé d'affaires. The American ambassador, Joseph Lake, was in Washington, DC, at the time, and it seemed that all of the other Western ambassadors were gone as well.

"Albania has just removed its highest judicial official, and they didn't follow the constitution," I said.

I showed him the hard evidence.

He paused before replying.

"We can't interfere with the internal politics of a sovereign nation," he said.

I looked at him with astonishment.

"I'll tell you what I will do," the chargé d'affaires said. "We have a consulate in Strasbourg, France, and I'm going to make an appointment with you to meet with the Council of Europe, which Albania has just joined."

On the same day, my last in Tirana, I had lunch with John Walker Jr., a cousin of President George W. Bush, at the outdoor cafe at the Pyramid. Charlie Waters, the deputy in charge of political affairs for the US Embassy, showed up.

Walker, a senior judge on the US Court of Appeals for the Second Circuit, made several trips to Albania to work on legal reform issues and teach judicial ethics. He worked with Albanian Presidents Aldred Moisiu and Bamir Topi, and Prime Ministers Fatos Nano and Sali Berisha, as well as Thimio and his successor as chief justice, Shpresa Becaj.

Charlie noted that two of his "friends," who had been tasked to follow him at all times, were at the table next to us. He made an appointment for me to meet at the White House with Richard Schifter, who at the time was a special assistant to President Clinton. From 1993 to 2001, Schifter served successively as counselor and senior director on the staff of the United States National Security Council and special adviser to the secretary of state.

In the meantime, I prepared to travel to Strasbourg for meetings on October 9 and 10 with the Council of Europe's general counsel and the general secretary.

A thought arose.

"Are they going to listen to a lawyer from Poulsbo, Washington, a town they've never heard of?

Bob Utter came to mind once again.

It just so happened that Bob was at a conference in The Hague on the topic of capital punishment. I called his wife, Betty, at their home in Olympia to see how I could reach him.

Every time I called Betty, she had an inkling that I was going to take Bob away from her. Earlier that year, when I called on him to help rescue the three justices, he missed her retirement party.

"Promise you won't take him away from me too long, Roger?"

She gave me his phone number in the Netherlands. Bob immediately understood the gravity of the moment and arranged for a flight from Amsterdam.

That evening, I picked him up from the airport and we went out to dinner. It was clear to us that Albania's future as a democracy was at stake.

"I think we're in Munich in 1938," I said. "We've got to uphold the rule of law."

First, we were vetted by the legal counsel for the Council of Europe, who asked us a lot of questions.

"Did Zef insult the president?" he asked.

We politely explained that Zef's criticism of President Berisha and of colleagues who were succumbing to the executive branch takeover of the judiciary are what we call freedom of petition and freedom of speech.

Finally, we met the general secretary.

"Would the Council of Europe say this was an improper removal of the highest judicial figure in the country, contrary to the constitution on several counts?" I asked.

"We do not expect these emerging democracies to be perfect, so we're not going to do anything," he said. "We need to maintain dialogue with them."

As we drove back to the airport, Bob said, "Now I know how World War II started."

We discussed the fact that nobody stood up to Hitler after he invaded the Sudetenland region of Czechoslovakia. After all, the Western powers reasoned, it was a German-speaking area, and Herr Hitler said there wouldn't be any more invasions.

THE MAN WE NEEDED TO MEET

I got on the plane to Washington, DC.

At the White House, while at the checkpoint on the corner of the grounds, who should be in the line with me but Wes Clark.

I hadn't seen him since graduation. At the time he was the commanding general of Southern Command.

"What are you here for, Rog?" he asked.

I told Wes, who at that time was on his way to becoming NATO commander, of the crisis in Albania.

"Well, that's interesting," he replied, "because I think I'm going to have some interest in Albania."

In the West Wing, near the Oval Office, I sat down with Dick Schifter, the special assistant to the president, in his office.

I put the first-hand evidence on his desk.

"This is amazing, all the information you got and the way you interpreted it," he said. "I'm going to show it to President Clinton."

There might have been no one better at the White House on the issues of liberty, justice, and human rights than Dick Schifter.

Born in Vienna in 1923 into a Jewish family that had fled Poland, Schifter emigrated to the United States after the Nazi annex of Austria in 1938.[22] He joined the US Army and became one of the famous Ritchie Boys, the young Jewish refugees whose German-language skills were used in intelligence work.

He was in the field during the Normandy landings and stationed in Aachen, Germany, after the Battle of the Bulge, where his interviews of the civilian population became part of one of the first studies of daily life under the Third Reich. After the war, he searched for his family.

They all had been killed in the Holocaust.

Before coming to the White House, Schifter represented the US in the United Nations Commission on Human Rights and served as deputy United States representative in the United Nations Security Council with the rank of ambassador.

During that time, he battled nations that ignored the human rights protections established by the UN Charter and used the charter instead to try to embarrass the US and delegitimize Israel. In 1985, President Ronald Reagan nominated Schifter to be assistant secretary of state for human rights and humanitarian affairs.

Schifter showed my information to President Clinton, and the US became the only nation to protest Zef's unlawful removal.

9

TELL THE WORLD

WHAT IS HAPPENING

TWO MONTHS LATER, I was in my Poulsbo office when a call came from Zef.

"They are about to arrest me. Tell the world what is happening," he said.

It was Saturday morning, November 5, 1995, and his apartment had been surrounded by police, both uniformed officers and members of the secret police, the SHIK.

The knock on his door came at 5 a.m.

Zef, reflecting later, said he knew there would be trouble after his speech at the July 1995 judicial conference chastising some of his fellow judges for becoming subservient to corrupt politicians, including receiving bribes.

"But I thought that if I don't act now, what we fought for in December 1990, to bring down the communist regime, would be for nothing," he said.

"The Albanian people were so thirsty for justice, for democracy. If I don't do my part, I can never feel good within myself."

The officers were at his door.

The plan we devised with the US Embassy went like this: Zef would call the embassy and say, "This is Zef Brozi, I want to speak to Carlo." Carlo was Carl Siebentritt, the political officer at the embassy. Before the call was even forwarded to Siebentritt, a car would be dispatched to Zef's apartment with an embassy representative, his passport and plane tickets.

"Hand over your passport," one officer demanded.

Zef, who was with his wife and 85-year-old mother, didn't open the door. His mother, visiting from Mirdita, was recovering from surgery. Through a camera that had been installed by his nephew, he watched the impatient officers.

"Do you have any authorization from the prosecutor or the court?" Zef asked through the locked door. They said no.

"Do you have any papers from the Ministry of Justice?" Zef followed. "No," they said.

"Who authorized you? Do you have an order?" Zef asked.

Again, the answer was no.

But they insisted that Zef open the door.

The US Embassy had advised Zef that if he were ever in danger, he could call them at any time.

"It was 5 a.m.," Zef said. "I didn't want to disturb the US Embassy or my friends. However, I knew the government could deny all that they were doing if I didn't have proof, so I called some journalists, members of Parliament, friends and lawyers."

Some came to his apartment and witnessed the scene.

At about 8 a.m., Diana called the US Embassy and a car soon arrived. The envoy found some humor in an otherwise grim situation.

He said that when the police saw his car with the American flag, they immediately tried to move their squad car. But it was stuck in the mud, and several officers had to get behind it and push.

With a representative of the United States of America present, Zef then agreed to hand over his diplomatic passport. But he did it on the condition that every detail be recorded and signed, including how many stamps and pages were in it and who was receiving it.

One parliamentary deputy who had come to Zef's aid called the minister of foreign affairs and said the police were demanding Zef's passport.

"Why are the police there for his passport? They have nothing to do with it," the minister said.

The deputy went outside and asked the chief of police to come in Zef's apartment and join the US Embassy representative, journalists, and others. Zef and his colleagues began writing down the details, crafting a statement for the passport, and gave it to the officer to sign.

The officer said, "No, I have to call my boss."

"You came at 5 in the morning and asked for the passport, asked to open the door. I didn't," Zef replied. "Now, I am giving you the passport, but you have to sign."

The officer made a phone call to his superior.

"No, don't get his passport," the boss said. "Let Zef come out and bring the passport."

Zef recalled, "I knew from the beginning, at 5 a.m. on Saturday, with so many police cars, secret police, and some criminals, that they were from Berisha's gang, and their intent was to make me disappear.

"They could have done that, and no one would have known what happened. Thank God I didn't open the door."

For the next week, with his apartment surrounded, he didn't go outside.

It so happened that when he was still chief justice, he had been invited to attend a conference in the United States by the Center for Democracy. He had sent another passport, his citizen passport, to the US Embassy to process the visa application. And it was still there.

NOT HAPPY TO LET ME GO

The embassy immediately began to execute the plan that had been in place since Zef was warned that Berisha wanted to stage a car "accident."

"This is Zef Brozi, I want to speak to Carlo," Zef said. A car was dispatched to Zef's apartment with an embassy representative, his passport, and plane tickets.

Zef told only close family members that he and Diana would be surreptitiously escorted to the airport by an embassy official early Sunday morning, November 12, and fly to the United States.

After living in a surveilled apartment for one week, Zef and Diana wondered what they might encounter at the airport.

"We had that kind of human fear," he said, "not because there was legal cause, but because of the evil of the president. He was not happy to let me go."

The plan went without a hitch—with the notable exception of the takeoff being aborted, as I recounted in Chapter 1, and the secret service officers in pursuit as the jet finally left Albanian soil.

The secret service, Shërbimi Informativ Kombëtar, or SHIK, was the successor to the Sigurimi, the notorious agency that Enver Hoxha used to brutally suppress dissent.

The broad public belief was that the SHIK was under Berisha's control as a political weapon.

Zef said he learned later, through officials close to Berisha who had left the country, that the president, indeed, "wanted to take us out."

By taking out, I asked Zef, do you mean he wanted to kill you and Diana?

"To take us out from the plane," he said. "Then I don't know what he wanted to do.

"I cannot put myself in evil's mind."

THE WORST PART OF DEMOCRACY

Zef said that when he helped lead the student movement that overthrew the communists in 1990, he and his allies thought "democracy was kind of easy."

"But we didn't know what democracy was. Unfortunately, those who left the Communist Party, they became the leaders of the opposition parties. All of them," Zef said.

"That was the worst part of democracy in Albania—the mentality of people, it's hard to change."

Zef said that after his removal, he initially thought Berisha no longer perceived him as a threat. Zef had planned to open a law office in Tirana and establish a nonprofit called the Rule of Law Foundation.

"We could have used that to train lawyers, judges, and prosecutors to do good," he said. "But still the president and the government saw me as a danger, because I had a reputation for organizing the youth and students."

He noted the joint effort of "Albanians and Americans working together" to help form an independent judiciary.

Zef had a major role in drafting the new constitution. He pointed out that experts from France and other European nations also took part.

"They said, 'Zef, your ideas are too American,'" he recalled, laughing.

"But I said, 'If America has the best ideas for the judiciary, why should we not learn from them?"

Zef said in an interview that it was "because of Roger and his team, I really became willing to stand up for the independence of the judiciary—and that brought me trouble.»

"That's the reason that, unfortunately, I became an immigrant in the United States. If I hadn't embraced American judicial independence, I could still be in Albania," said Zef.

He said he never wanted to leave Albania.

"But you cannot fight with everyone. It was not the right time for justice in Albania."

He had only a handful of allies in the judiciary at the time who were willing to press for its independence.

"They can plant seeds, but it is not easy to change the situation or the mentality," Zef observed.

DEJA VU ALL OVER AGAIN

Months after Zef's departure, and four years after Albania's first free elections, Human Rights Watch/Helsinki issued a bleak report as the Balkan nation prepared for parliamentary elections in May 1996.

Berisha was seeking reelection, the global watchdog said, and the country had yet to "establish a democracy with full respect for human rights."

"The Stalinist nature of Albania's past and its legacy of one-party rule were reflected in the government's ongoing attempt to silence its critics, Human Rights Watch said.[23] "Political trials, media campaigns and police violence were all used against members of the political opposition, as well as against others who expressed views different from the state."

Reminders of the past were rekindled after authorities arrested Hoxha's successor and onetime right-hand man, Ramiz Alia, on February 1, 1996, and charged him with the internment and imprisonment in concentration camps of thousands of citizens during the communist regime.[24] Later, Alia was charged with ordering the killing of people who attempted to leave the country; ordering troops and police to fire on the people who toppled the Hoxha monument in Tirana in early 1991; ordering the arming of military students who subsequently killed some civilians; and other counts. Previously, however, a Tirana court dismissed charges against him of genocide and crimes against humanity.

Ahead of the elections, more remnants of the past came to life as the Albanian media came under increased attack from the government. Police arbitrarily detained journalists, confiscating material and film. Two journalists were convicted of slandering government officials, one of whom was banned from participating in politics or writing publicly for one year.

In November 1995, a bomb destroyed the home of the publisher of Koha Jonë, Nikolle Lesi. Two months later, the government confiscated four distribution vans owned by the newspaper, insisting the vehicles had been registered improperly. The paper shot back, declaring the seizure was because of its unwillingness to back the Democratic Party ahead of the elections.

A week later, another Koha Jonë journalist was arrested, allegedly for assaulting two policemen.

Human Rights Watch said that of particular concern was the executive branch's continued intrusions on the independence of the judiciary.

Berisha's effort to block Zef's review of the controversial case of Socialist Party leader Fatos Nano became an election issue. Nano was sentenced to prison in July 1993 on charges of "embezzlement of state property to the benefit of third persons" and "falsification of official documents" amid protests from numerous human rights organizations and the Council of Europe.

Another opposition leader, Idajet Beqiri, was sentenced to fifteen years' imprisonment on charges of "crimes against humanity."

Amnesty International studied their cases and concluded that the charges were not substantiated by the evidence produced in court and were politically motivated.[25]

In other words, the human rights group said, "they were convicted on false charges as a way of punishing them for their non-violent political activities."

Berisha won an overwhelming victory. But the official tally clearly did not reflect the will of the people. Despite the government's effort to control the media, Albanians had rejected the Democratic Party.

VOTE EARLY, VOTE OFTEN

I sent a fax to James Bigus of the Bureau of Human Rights in the US State Department on May 30, 1996, to follow up a telephone conversation regarding the clear evidence that Berisha had stolen the election.

The conduct of the vote and actions leading to it "should raise serious doubts about the current Albanian leadership," I wrote.

I noted that I had been closely involved with Albania for the previous four years, leading several teams of US judges and lawyers to assist the Albanian judiciary. During that time, I had become acquainted with members of the government, numerous deputies of the Parliament, all the members of the Albanian Supreme Court and more than one hundred other Albanian judges and journalists. I had met with President Berisha many times, and spoken on Albanian radio and television and the Voice of America on behalf of the proposed constitution.

My letter, I explained, was based on those experiences and contacts, and on recent telephone and email communication with reliable sources in Albania.

"Sunday's election was the culmination of an extended and well-planned effort to ensure the continuation of the current leadership in Albania," I wrote. "From several Albanian sources it has been reported to me that ballot boxes were stuffed, and ballots were changed in a variety of ways to favor the Democratic Party. Police and soldiers at polling places intimidated voters."

There was a clear, widespread pattern of tampering with ballot boxes, suggesting an orchestrated plan to ensure votes for Democratic Party candidates.

I had several reports that election commission officials, including at local levels, were controlled by government employees.

A reliable Western observer in Albania reported the following eyewitness examples of election abuses:

In at least twelve voting zones, Democratic Party members in charge of ballot boxes arrived at the voting polls with ballot boxes already stuffed with ballots;

Many people were observed placing multiple ballots in the ballot boxes, some with as many as eighty to ninety ballots;

University students recruited by the Democratic Party to stuff ballot boxes joked that the Democratic Party may end up with more than 110 percent of the vote;

In the university housing area, many people were seen voting multiple times, bringing in five ballots each time;

Incorrect ballots were provided to voters and then replaced with ballots favoring the Democratic Party;

In certain areas, ballots were printed in a format to cause confusion. This was done particularly in rural areas where the educational level is low;

At Voting Center 13 of Zone 94, many people were seen voting five or six times during the day;

In Voting Center 15 of Zone 93, six young men entered the Voting Center violently and placed more than two hundred ballots in the box; their car had a Tirana license plate;

In 15 Voting Centers of Zone 16, there were major violations where people voted more than ten times;

In at least one Voting Center, the Election Commission was comprised only of Democratic Party members;

At more than 80 percent of the voting locations, people were placed by the Democratic Party to intimidate voters.

BRUTAL CONTEMPT

I reported to Bigus that the violence that took place following the election in the main square of Tirana underscored the contempt that the Albanian leadership had for the democratic process.

The violence appeared to have been directed at leaders of minority parties. Several reliable sources reported that among the many injured by the police was Arben Imami, a leader of the Democratic Alliance. He was beaten and left unconscious, losing teeth, and remained seriously injured.

Observers reported other police brutality against an otherwise peaceful demonstration in the main square of Tirana. And there was a report that the minister of the interior, who controls the police, was personally in the square beating people. A doctor saw him and reminded him of his duty. The minister then started beating the doctor and took him to the police station.

I gave the State Department official a list of prominent persons and others who were the victims of police violence surrounding the election:

Arben Imami of the Democratic Alliance suffered a broken jaw, four broken teeth, and severe clubbing to the kidney and chest;

Arben Imami's wife was beaten severely and jailed;

Namik Dokle of the Socialist Party;

Gramoz Pashko of the Democratic Alliance (formerly in the Democratic Party);

Skender Gjnushi of the Social Democratic Party;

Paskel Milo of the Social Democratic Party;

Gaqo Apostoli of the Social Democratic Party. (The incident was also seen on Euro News and NBC);

Pandeli Majko of the Social Democratic Party was beaten so badly he had to be carried. He was also taken to the police station and held for numerous hours;

Andre Legisi of the Socialist Party suffered a large cut above his eye and multiple bruises;

Servet Pellumbi, the vice president of the Socialist Party, was beaten so badly that four people had to carry him;

Two women were beaten so severely that it was believed by witnesses that they were dead. No further report was available, as later they could not be found;

One Spanish journalist and more than one British journalist were beaten, arrested, and taken to a jail where they were beaten again;

K. Gjipali, a member of the voting commission for Zone 47 in Tirana. Police came and started beating him for no reason at the voting site, arrested him and held him in jail for more than seven hours;

Erion Brace, a journalist for the Socialist newspaper. When Brace got into his car on Sunday, two men were hiding in the back seat. They pushed a gun to his head and told him to drive to the city of Berat. They told him he could not write articles against President Berisha;

Shpetim Hyka reported voting discrepancies at Voting Center 15 in Zone 93 to the head of the Voting Commission; he was then arrested violently and taken to a local jail. There were hundreds of other similar cases with normal citizens;

Two Associated Press journalists filming the events in Skanderbeg Square were struck with riot batons, arrested, and taken to the police station;

Several foreign journalists were picked up and had all their film confiscated;

Blendi Gonxhe, who was one of the leaders of the university student protests in 1990, was beaten on the street. (Apparently this was shown on Euro News). He was then taken to an underground jail cell where he was beaten until unconscious. Blendi is reported to have said he was returning the medal he was awarded for bravery back to the president's office. Blendi also reported that when in prison he saw several foreign reporters and noticed many Albanian women were there.

'STRONG AND DECISIVE ACTION'

Meanwhile, from exile in the United States, Zef signed a faxed letter to US Secretary of State Warren Christopher urging the United States to withdraw recognition of the results and call for a new election.

Zef said the May 26 elections took place "in a psychological and physical climate of terror that the neodictatorial power of Berisha exercised upon the main opposition parties during the electoral campaign."

The former Albanian chief justice said it "now appears that the abuses on election day itself far exceeded our expectations and erase any doubt that Berisha will do whatever is necessary to stay in power."

After the elections already had begun, Berisha changed the ballots and postponed the time to end voting from 8 p.m., as the law requires, to 10 p.m.

"These actions have been conducted so that the votes could be falsified by the Democratic Party," Zef wrote.

"The Albanian people know the truth of these matters, but because of our recent history will find it easy to be silent," he said. "Should the United States and Western Europe, however, speak out and call for new elections, the people of Albania will know they have the support of those who can help them."

I concluded my May 30, 1996, memo to Bigus with a similar sense of gravity.

"What happens next in Albania will be determined by the response of the US and Western Europe," I wrote. "If we acknowledge the elections as valid, then democracy has little or no chance in Albania and human rights and basic freedoms will be denied."

I noted that Albanians "remember and fear the repressive regime of their past" but they could easily fall to a new one.

"If on the other hand we take strong and decisive action it will give hope and encouragement to the Albanian people and many leaders who genuinely seek to establish the Rule of Law and fundamental human rights."

THE MIRACLE OF EDUART SELAMI

I put all the evidence that Berisha had rigged the election in a memo and sent it to the White House and the State Department. I sanitized it enough so that individuals would not get into trouble if it got back to Albania,

A few days later, I received a call from Dick Schifter at the White House.

"Roger, I believe everything in your letter," he said. "But I just wanted to let you know that we probably won't do anything. We rarely go behind a democratic election."

He noted that the US had protested a foreign election only twice since World War II.

"This just isn't enough," he said.

"Dick, what does it take?" I asked. "This is black and white; we are installing a dictator in Albania, and we are doing it on your watch."

After speaking those words, I thought to myself, "Sherrard, watch what you are saying; you are talking to the White House. You probably should be a little more respectful."

Schifter was a gracious man.

"Well, Roger, I appreciate everything you are saying, and I believe it, but it just probably isn't going to happen," he replied.

"Dick, what would it take?" I asked. "What would you need?"

"Well, in this case, we would need a credible Albanian politician to come to Washington, DC, and verify what's in your memo," he said.

"There's not much I can do," Schifter continued. "Unless you have an insider who can come and testify here before our Albania focus group on Wednesday."

The committee, chaired by Schifter, was composed of officials from the State Department, the Department of Defense, and other agencies who had an interest in Albania.

It was Monday. Finding an "insider" was one challenge. Putting him before the panel two days later was quite another.

Dejected, I hung up the phone.

How in the world would I ever get someone from Albania to testify to the committee in time?

It was already about 5 p.m. in Washington, DC.

I immediately tried to call several people in Albania, but the international lines were busy.

About fifteen minutes after I had hung up the phone with Dick Schifter, my secretary, Linda Wood, walked into my office.

"There's somebody on the phone for you," she said. "I think his name is something like 'salami.' He sounds European or Albanian."

My heart leaped. Eduart Selami had been a close adviser to Berisha and the chairman of the Democratic Party. When he criticized Berisha for removing Zef, he became persona non grata and was ousted as chairman on March 5, 1995.[26]

At the time of the call, he was still a member of the Parliament of Albania.

I exclaimed, "He's the perfect person to testify!"

Linda began humming the "doo-do doo-do doo-do doo-do" theme from the old *Twilight Zone* television series. It had become her signature way of suggesting that, once again, something extraordinary, against all odds, was in the works.

I picked up the phone.

"Eduart, where are you?"

"I'm in Boston."

"What are you doing in Boston?"

He explained that after his ouster, he knew Berisha would continue to consolidate his power, so he accepted a Fulbright Scholarship that had been on the table for him for some time.

"I came here because I could see that things were getting too intense," he said.

Eduart is fluent in English and very smooth.

Before I could get in another word, he said, "You need to tell somebody what happened with the election."

I explained that I had just been on the phone with Dick Schifter in the White House, and Dick was looking for someone precisely like him.

"Can you be in Washington tomorrow?" I asked.

He said, "Tomorrow is the only day I can. I am leaving for Stanford University on Saturday."

"We'll get you a ticket," I replied. "I need to hang up now and call you back shortly. I need to call Schifter back right away."

It already was after-hours in the nation's capital. I tried the number

I had for Schifter anyway. I didn't realize it, but he had given me his inside line that rings at his desk after hours. He answered my call directly.

"How would Eduart Selami do?" I asked.

"You're kidding," Dick replied.

"Roger, I don't know how you do it!"

I called Eduart back and we worked out the details. Sam Ericsson met him at the airport and took him to the White House.

The members of the committee knew of Eduart. He had held the post of chairman of the Democratic Party while Berisha was in fact the head of the party. Previously under the law, the president, as head of state, could not belong to a political party. But Berisha's supporters persuaded Parliament to change the law and allow the president to be a member of a party as long as he was not the party's head.

Berisha, nevertheless, remained the de facto Democratic Party leader, and the precedent effectively made Parliament subservient to the executive.

About four days after Eduart's testimony, Schifter called me.

"We have changed our policy on Albania, and we are not going to honor the election," he said.

The US stood alone in protesting the election. Germany, France, Italy, and every other Western nation decided that while they didn't like Berisha, it was less costly to accept the results.

Washington received a lot of flak for its decision, with the US ambassador being shunned in Tirana for a time. But the American protest had teeth. Berisha's victory was nullified, and he agreed to an internationally monitored redo election in 1997.

Meanwhile, back home in Poulsbo, we faced a series of trials that threatened to derail not only the work in Albania but the law firm itself.

In July 1996, one of my partners was charged with embezzling funds from the firm.[27] Our pain was compounded by the division it caused among the partners. Some had wanted to prosecute, while others did not. And eventually three partners chose to resign. Then, in July 1998, our main office on Front Street was destroyed by a fire.[28]

The cause of the blaze was proven to be arson. But to this day, we don't know who did it. Our immediate concern was the condition of our clients' smoke- and water-damaged files, and the impact on our work. A foreboding washed over me when a client called and demanded that his files be brought to the front desk so he could take his business elsewhere. I told him my first problem was that we no longer had a front desk. As I began contemplating a flood of clients demanding the same thing, my secretary, Linda Wood, came to me with a box of files asking what should be done with the documents. It so happened that they were the files of the client who had just called. We handed over his papers in the parking lot. Typically, in such situations, a firm would lose many of its clients, but we lost only a few.

We received a wonderful outpouring of support from the community, including help to triage the documents. Remarkably, the Pacific Northwest received not a single day of rain from July to October, and we were able to bring tables full of soggy papers outside every day to dry them in the sun. In the meantime, we were up and running in rented offices nearby. While I had insurance to cover any interruption of business, we didn't have to use it. We were blessed with a bigger year financially than the previous one.

When we returned to our restored building, Linda hung a plaque on my office wall that she had made. It featured Scripture verses—I Peter 1:6,7—in calligraphy:

In this you greatly rejoice, though now for a little while you may have had to suffer grief in various trials so that the proven character of your faith— more precious than gold, which perishes even though refined by fire—may result in praise, glory, and honor at the revelation of Jesus Christ

10

EASY MONEY

IN ALBANIA, it was not a smooth path from protesting and nullifying the May 1996 elections to holding new elections in 1997. The year began with a revolt that some describe as a civil war or a period of anarchy that teetered on civil war.

In the transition from a Stalinist command economy to a market-based economy, government officials were lured by the quick fix of pyramid investment funds, otherwise known as Ponzi schemes. In simple terms, payments to old investors were made using money contributed by new investors.

Some two-thirds of the Albanian population, who were making an average of about $80 a month, participated in the Ponzi schemes. Many handed over life savings and even sold their homes at the prospect of immediate high returns. Kiosks sprang up all over the country where people lined up to hand over their cash and—for a time—reap astonishing monthly interest rates of from 10 to 25 percent. It was estimated that a total of $1.5 billion was invested in the schemes, many of which became fronts for laundering money and arms trafficking.

But as with all such schemes, when the pool of new investors runs out, so does the money to keep paying the previous investors. By January 1997, the payments largely had stopped, and Albanians, who had lost a total of $1.2 billion, took to the streets.[29]

Anarchy followed, with daily protests of angry citizens charging they had been duped by the government. On March 1, Prime Minister Aleksandër Meksi resigned, and a day later, Berisha declared a state of emergency, banning public gatherings of more than four people and imposing a curfew.

On the first night of the emergency, the office of the anti-Berisha paper Koha Jonë was ransacked and burned. Pro-Democratic Party forces were widely assumed to be responsible, although Koha Jonë was unable to present evidence.

On March 11, Berisha appointed the Socialist Party's leader, Bashkim Fino, as prime minister in a desperate bid for calm. But the protests spread to northern Albania. The government lost control, particularly in the south, which was taken over by rebels and criminal gangs. The entire country was engulfed in demonstrations by mid-March, and the US and other foreign nations began evacuating their citizens.

That month, every prisoner throughout the country escaped. (Later, the silver lining was that it gave the government the opportunity to rebuild and reconstruct prisons and jails to meet international standards).

The rebellion was not merely a showdown between the two main political forces but also Albania's two main ethnic subgroups, the Ghegs and the Tosks. The Ghegs, who speak a different dialect of Albanian, live in the mountainous north and in neighboring Kosovo, North Macedonia, Serbia, and Montenegro. The Islamic Ottomans took over the Tosk-inhabited south in the fifteenth century while mainly leaving the isolated Ghegs to themselves.

The communist regime created a standard Albanian language based on Tosk Albanian, imposing it on the anti-communist north.

Critics said the regime deprived the Albanian language of its richness, describing the language produced by the communists as a "monstrosity."

The Ghegs sided with Berisha, while the southerners, the ethnic Tosks, supported the Socialist Party.

On one side of the conflict in 1997 were the rebels, the Socialist Party, armed civilians who lost their properties, Albanian Army defectors, monarchists, and armed gangs from Southern Albania

On the other was the Berisha government and his Democratic Party along with armed gangs from Northern Albania, SHIK, a portion of the Albanian Police, and the Republican Guard, a militarized government agency that provides security for high-ranking state officials.

Berisha opened government weapons depots in the north, allowing civilians to arm themselves against the violence of the south. In the south, civilians had looted army bases. It was believed that nearly every male older than age ten had at least one firearm along with ammunition.

Along with 656,000 weapons and 1.5 billion rounds of ammunition, an estimated 3.5 million hand grenades and 1 million landmines were looted from army depots.

More than two thousand people were killed, and many more were wounded during the first six months of 1997, according to unofficial estimates, the US State Department said in a report.[30]

STARTING OVER

On June 29, the Socialist Party won one hundred seats out of 155 in the Parliament, which elected its secretary general, Rexhep Meidani, as president. Fatos Nano became the new prime minister.

Meidani promised to restore order and outlaw the pyramid schemes. But the killings and injuries continued throughout the year. Most deaths were due to accidents, whether from firearms or grenades, as armories were looted. Many intentional deaths, however, resulted from acts of revenge, from traditional blood feuds, or from fighting among rival criminal groups. Some deaths also reportedly resulted from insurgent attacks on the police or SHIK.

The judicial system was further undermined by the chaos and was unable to function in many places. Many of the court buildings were vandalized or burned down. Some judges were intimidated by the fact that criminals they had sentenced were freed.

Sam Ericsson already had a relationship with Meidani through a remarkable circumstance. But we didn't know what to make of the Socialist Party, knowing it was the successor to the communists.

Then, on July 29, a colleague in my Poulsbo office read out loud an email listing the new members of government, and there was a big shout.

Many of the new officials were our friends, including Thimio Kondi, the new minister of justice.

Thimio, who had embraced from the beginning the principles we were teaching, had resigned quietly from the Constitutional Court in late 1994 because he opposed Berisha's control of the court.

At that time, I told him that Albania needed men of courage. Don't go underground, I said. Your time will come. Be ready. I gave him the quote from Jeremy Bentham, the British philosopher, "When enough good men do nothing, evil prevails."

And now Thimio was the minister of justice.

I wrote him a letter of congratulations. I said that we would be praying for wisdom and guidance. I didn't say courage, though, but I had it in mind.

HERE, YOU TAKE HIM

Our relationship with Meidani began the previous December when, as the new Socialist Party leader, he came to Washington. Nobody wanted to talk to him, because he was the head of the biggest party in opposition to Berisha.

So, Dick Schifter called me and asked if we could get someone who could host him and take him around Washington.

Sam picked him up from the airport and was with him for the entire stay, inviting him to dinner at his home. They became good friends.

The leader of the Socialist Party was now the president of Albania.

Meidani was a physics professor at the University of Tirana who said he got involved in active politics only in response to the collapse of the pyramid investment schemes. Considered one of the country's top academics, he held PhDs from the University of Paris XI and the University of Tirana.

In August 1996, he was elected as the party's secretary-general. He said he understood that it was because there was an internal political conflict, and they needed someone from the outside.

Meidani said that in the wake of the pyramid schemes, his main concern was to rebuild trust between citizens and political leaders and to transform a destroyed country into a peaceful and democratic one.

He invited Sam to come to Tirana and meet him in his new presidential office. Sam invited me to join him for an August 13, 1997, meeting.

On August 1, Katoo and I were praying, and I said, "God, if you really want me to go, send me another letter." I came to the office and there was a letter from Thimio. We made the reservations.

'YOU SAID THERE WOULD BE A TIME'

Sam and I linked up in Zurich and took the two-hour flight to Tirana. From the US to Zurich, I got five hours of sleep on the plane. That had never happened before, and I arrived rested and ready to go despite the nine-hour time difference.

We arrived at Rinas Airport in Tirana, and Petrit was there with a car from the Supreme Court. Vjollca Proni's husband also came to pick us. Vjollca was visiting us in Poulsbo in 1994 when she found out that she was pregnant with her first child. We also were met at the airport by Thimio Kondi, who came in a Ministry of Justice car. We had three cars for two people.

At the hotel, Thimio insisted that we have dinner with him and his wife, Alexandra.

"Then we will plan the rest of your week," he said. "I want you to know you have a Ministry of Justice car, driver, and aide at your disposal the whole time you are here."

We had a brand-new Toyota 4-Runner with blue privacy curtains in the back and VIP license plates. Our driver-escort was an Army captain in civilian clothes.

We had a wonderful dinner that night with Thimio and Alexandra. He reminded me of the discussion we had had two and a half years before about courage.

"You said there would be a time . . . and now I need to have courage and be strong," he said.

Thimio told us he planned to introduce us to all the department heads in the Ministry of Justice.

"You should not have to ask for anything while you are here," he said. "They should provide whatever you want."

The next morning, we had a meeting scheduled with President Meidani at 10 a.m. Thimio briefed us. Usually, we had to hire translators as well as a car and driver, so this was like night and day for us.

We arrived at Meidani's office where we were greeted by aides who escorted us to his office. He welcomed Sam with open arms.

"The worst thing about being president is that I don't have any free time to do things with friends anymore," said Meidani, who spoke English fluently. "My wife can't go out for coffee."

THE FOUNDATION FOR GOVERNING

We had a great discussion about Meidani's vision for his presidency. He wanted his government to be a government of reconciliation. They would not put all their enemies in jail as was done in the previous administration.

He emphasized governing by the right principles and recited the Golden Rule to us, saying it must become the foundation for government.

"Now, I want to have an independent judiciary. We've got big problems with the judiciary," he said.

I said, "Yes, we are aware of that, and we are here to help you. We know there are some delicate problems."

"What do you mean delicate problems?" the president asked. "You mean corruption?"

"Yes, and we have some ideas to deal with it," I replied.

As we concluded, he said, "We aren't done yet.

"I want you to come to my home at 4 o'clock and meet my wife and children. We have more to discuss."

I connected with Meidani personally, and eventually we became like brothers. We both were born in August 1944 and are about the same height. On a subsequent visit, the president and I had a debate about who was the tallest. We stood back-to-back, and it appeared that he was the winner. But later it was revealed that he had stood on his toes.

That kind of «corruption» was all in fun. But Meidani understood the corruption that Albania faced, calling it "capillary corruption.» By that he meant corruption was in the ancient nation's bloodstream.

There's the nurse who wants a cash payment before administering a shot. The university professor who sells an improved grade for $100. The telephone service supervisor who demands $1,500 under the table before you can even begin ordering a phone for your home.

Politically, we didn't see eye to eye. He once told me that he thought the government should guarantee everyone a job. I told him I didn't think that would work out well.

'WILLIAM COLBY OWES ME A HUSBAND'

We then headed for a meeting with the head of a newly created ministry-level position, the minister of government reorganization.

And who should that new minister be but Arben Armani, the Parliament member who gave us the affidavit proving there was not a quorum in Parliament when Zef was removed.

"Our first plan is to deal with government corruption," he said. "And the second is to rewrite the constitution."

Zef, who had been serving with Advocates International in the US as a judicial fellow for the previous six months, was working on a revision of the constitution.

We had good meetings with Arben and several other government leaders on our first day and the next morning. They all expressed appreciation to the United States for being the only Western nation to protest the election. They respected us for taking a stand that was unpopular.

That night we had dinner with Kozara Koti of the Albanian Human Rights Documentation Center, who had helped us when Parliament was trying to expel the three judges. She formed the human rights group to help political dissidents who had been persecuted under the communist regime. Susana Frasheri, a judge who had been illegally removed, joined us for dinner.

Kozara's father had been a political prisoner, sent to prison on a false accusation that he was a CIA agent.

She quipped, "William Colby owes me a husband, because my husband divorced me when my father was charged." Colby was the director of the CIA in the mid-1970s.

It turned out that the new president, Meidani, had been the chairman of the board of her organization.

"My job for the next five years is to make sure neither one of those guys gets a big head," she said of Meidani and the new prime minister, Fatos Nano.

She expressed skepticism that even the people she knew and trusted could turn things around.

The next morning, we had a meeting with Nano, the Socialist Party leader who had been sentenced to prison in July 1993 on charges of "embezzlement of state property to the benefit of third persons" and "falsification of official documents" amid protests from numerous human rights organizations and the Council of Europe. Berisha's effort to block Zef Brozi's review of Nano's controversial case was an issue in the June election.

Before leaving for Albania on this trip, I had come across some old photographs and discovered that I had taken a shot of the Supreme Court when it was hearing the case of a political dissident. I put the photo in my briefcase on a whim.

The dissident was Fatos Nano.

The court's ruling in favor of Nano's constitutional rights was a turning point for Zef Brozi as well, leading to the loss of his position as chief justice. But it also was the beginning of the end for Berisha, as he became more and more dictatorial. Berisha removed Zef so that the court could not finalize that case.

"Mr. Prime Minister, I just happen to have a picture of the court on the day it argued your case," I said. "We were there for that argument. As you can see, the date is stamped on the picture."

"You know one of the turning points was the day the court decided to hear my case," Nano told me.

He served three years in prison.

"I wasn't in prison as long as Nelson Mandela, but I am going to fashion my leadership after his," Nano said. "We are only going to do what we have to do. We are not going to retaliate and take revenge on people."

He said that while in prison, there were only two books to read. One of them was the Bible.

"I read it through thirteen times, and I know what you stand for," he said.

In parting, he gave us a copy of the Albanian Government Program in English. He wrote in it, "To the right partners and the right time for starting a new future for Albania. Fatos Nano. August 13, 1997"

Nano, who grew up in Tirana, graduated from a high school reserved for the children of the nomenklatura, the communist ruling class.[31] But he began to develop an interest in learning foreign languages and played the guitar. He was the lead singer in a rock group he founded that played the strictly forbidden music of the Beatles. He graduated from the University of Tirana in 1978 and in 1984 was appointed as a researcher at the Institute of Marxist-Leninist Studies in Tirana, where he worked until 1990. During that time, he was singled out by Enver Hoxha's wife, Nexhmije Hoxha, who followed his career and helped him move up the ladder.

In the wake of the revolutions throughout Eastern Europe, Enver Hoxha's personally selected successor, Ramiz Alia, appointed Nano in February 1991 as prime minister of a transitional government to organize the first post-communist democratic elections. When the communists, the Labour Party of Albania, won the March 31, 1991, elections, Alia again appointed Nano as prime minister. But one week later, after a general strike organized by the newly independent unions, Nano was forced to resign. In June 1991, the Labour Party changed its name to the Socialist Party, expelled all the members of the politburo, and elected Nano as the new leader of the Socialist Party.

'We will hold the plane' Petrit had made an appointment with Zef's replacement as chief justice of the Supreme Court, Avni Shehu, who in the two times we had seen him since Zef's removal had been very distant and cold.

Avni knew that Zef was a good friend of mine and that I had been the best man in Zef's wedding. Petrit was with me.

As the meeting progressed, Avni warmed up. At the end of our time, he wrote in a book, "For a sign of gratitude for your assistance to the Albanian Judiciary. Chief Justice Avni Shehu."

He then showed us around the court. The library had been completed, and it included all the books we had presented to them over the previous four years.

My meeting with Avni went overtime. But Petrit said there were four friends of Zef's who were demanding to take me to lunch.

"I have to get out to the airport and catch my plane," I protested.

But one of Zef's friends, Agim Hoxha, a lawyer in Tirana with a strong bearing, was insistent.

"We will hold the plane. You must come to lunch with us," he said. "What do you say?"

We went to lunch.

They were very appreciative, thanking us for all we had done for Zef and for Albania.

They all decided to escort us to the airport. We left the restaurant behind police cars with sirens blaring, swerving around ox charts and run-down Mercedes, and blasting through jarring chuckholes.

They whisked us through the VIP section of the airport. We didn't have to check in. And in no time we were out on the tarmac and heading up the stairs to our plane as they waved goodbye.

REAWAKENING

Sam's relationship with Meidani turned out to be crucial in another major crisis in Albania. The trouble began in March 1999, when NATO launched a military air strike in neighboring Kosovo that provoked a wave of ethnic Albanian refugees.

It was during that time that Sam introduced Meidani to the reemergent evangelical church in Albania, which had been violently erased from public life along with all other expressions of faith during the Hoxha era.

Meidani said that if it weren't for the evangelicals filling in the gaps during the refugee crisis, the whole thing could have blown up.

The government authorities had almost no experience in refugee matters and limited resources. Nearly 435,000 refugees left Kosovo for Albania, according to the United Nations High Commissioner for Refugees, the UNHCR. At the height of the bombing, refugees were crossing the border into Albania at the rate of four thousand per hour. Afterward, the UNHCR stated that up to 25 percent of the population of Kosovo had fled.[32]

In 1991, fewer than two dozen known evangelical Protestant believers remained from the church that existed before the communist takeover. Just six years later, there were more than 120 churches throughout the country. They had an outsized influence, much like the nineteenth century founder of the modern evangelical movement in Albania, Gjerasim Qiriazi, who is regarded as one of the country's great patriots and heroes.

The churches, with the support of a network of foreign missions called the Albanian Encouragement Project, immediately mobilized hundreds of volunteers who organized transit centers for the refugees in every major town and city in the country. The refugees were fed, registered, and taken in by families or housed in camps.

In the first two weeks of the crisis, despite representing only one-half of 1 percent of the population, evangelical churches handled nearly 80 percent of the arriving refugees. And for months, they continued to provide help, earning the respect and gratitude of officials.

President Meidani praised the evangelicals in an official statement.

"I wish to acknowledge the Evangelical believers of Albania for the dedication and service rendered to tens of thousands of Kosovar refugees during one of the most difficult chapters in the history of our nation," he wrote.

"Throughout the country these believers exemplified faith in action through their practical application of the Golden Rule, 'Do unto others as you would have them do unto you.'"

Meidani said that "in this they have shown their determination to continue in the tradition of men like Gjerasim Qiriazi, who lived to serve his nation in the hope of making this world a better place."

Born in 1858, Qiriazi, the son of a poor carpenter, become a scholar and a key leader in Albania's *Rilindja*, or "National Awakening," as it is known.[33] He faced fierce opposition, including in 1884, when he was kidnapped by bandits and held for six months.

The Qiriazi family is known in Albania for its contribution to the Albanian language, literature, and education. Gjerasim Qiriazi and his sisters founded an Albanian school for girls in 1891 that was ground-breaking in a predominantly Islamic culture in which women were not formally educated.

Qiriazi believed that educating future mothers was the quickest way to transform a society. He hoped that they would produce a culture better than the one that produced the brigands who held him.

Education in the Albanian language was forbidden under the Ottoman Empire, and there was no commonly accepted Albanian alphabet. Now, the Qiriazi family is named in every Albanian history textbook as pioneers of the Albanian language and leaders of the country's "national renaissance."

In 1892, Gjerasim Qiriazi led the first Albanian evangelicals in the formation of a network of churches called the Evangelical Brotherhood, the *Vellazeria Ungjillore.*

During the communist era, a movie was made about the first girls' school, but there was no mention of the faith that inspired and guided it.

The Vellazeria Ungjillore e Shqiperise, the Evangelical Brotherhood of Albania, was officially recognized by the government in 2011 as the fifth faith group, after Orthodox and Roman Catholic churches, Sunni Islam, and the Bektashi.

11

UNLIMITED POWER

WITH SALI BERISHA'S DEMOCRATIC PARTY IN POWER, the Albanian Parliament drafted a Constitution in 1994 that was "designed to give unlimited power to the president of the republic," the opposition parties charged.

The draft constitution, the opposition further contended, also "failed to contain full guarantees for the impartiality of the judiciary system." And in November 1994, the document was rejected in a referendum of the people, with 54 percent opposed and 43 percent in favor.

After the popular vote, the four top opposition parties called for adopting a new draft constitution "the legal way." That is, they pointed out, by requiring that it pass a parliamentary committee, then a vote in Parliament, and, finally, ratification by the people through a referendum.

The opposition parties—the Democratic Alliance, Union of Human Rights, the Social-Democratic Party, and the Socialist Party—noted that their proposal for drafting a new constitution was supported by some deputies of the Democratic Party. Among them was Eduart Selami, who later provided the crucial testimony in Washington, DC, that led to the US protesting the 1997 election.

But during a called special meeting, the Democratic Party removed Selami from his post as party president. It was during that emergency meeting that Berisha and other leaders decided that the constitution would not be addressed until the 1997 session of the legislature.

WE, THE PEOPLE OF ALBANIA

Members of Parliament invited us to participate in the drafting of the constitution. Justice Utter put together a team of advisers. I testified three times in 1997 before the drafting committee and regularly exchanged comments.

I wanted to see the Golden Rule somehow expressed in the preamble to the Constitution. I proposed language derived from our Declaration of Independence, "We are endowed by our creator with certain inalienable rights."

That fundamental declaration was not in the final version, although there is a reference to the divine, stating that the constitution is established "with faith in God and/or other universal values."

The preamble reads:

We, the people of Albania, proud and aware of our history, with responsibility for the future, and with faith in God and/or other universal values,

with determination to build a social and democratic state based on the rule of law, and to guarantee the fundamental human rights and freedoms,

with a spirit of tolerance and religious coexistence,

with the pledge for the protection of human dignity and personhood, as well as for the prosperity of the whole nation, for peace, well-being, culture and social solidarity, with the centuries-old aspiration of the Albanian people for national identity and unity,

with a deep conviction that justice, peace, harmony and cooperation among nations are among the highest values of humanity,

We establish this Constitution

Significantly, like the US Constitution, Article 2 of the Albanian constitution states that sovereignty belongs to the Albanian people. And it establishes a separation of powers, with three branches of government.

The Albanians ended up with a compromise between European continental law, and the British and American common law. The British philosophy, which the United States has adopted, is based on the rule of law, legal precedent, and trial by jury. Continental law emphasizes a codified set of core principles that serve as the primary source of law.

I believe we built credibility through the annual seminars. And when it came time to write the religious freedom provision of the law and the constitution, our testimony was given great weight.

The initial draft religion law in 1993 gave the Albanian government the power to oversee religious institutions and ensure they don't violate "the constitution, the laws or the national interests" of the state. And it required the Albanian president to approve the appointment of the top leaders of religious communities. The US urged Parliament not to endorse the provisions and they were dropped in October 1993. The constitution drafted in 1997 prohibits any official religion and makes the state neutral regarding religious belief, recognizing the equality and independence of religious groups. And it prohibits discrimination based on religion.

Bob and I also introduced American public disclosure laws to Albania, which require that judges in public office fill out income and asset forms. We took it one step further than American laws, requiring that the disclosures be published in a newspaper. And if a judicial candidate does not report assets, those assets will be subject to confiscation by the government.

All the ideas we presented, of course, had to be woven into Albania's culture.

There are some good things they included in their laws that we don't have. If I write a letter to my son, for example, it's private property under Albanian law. You can't use personal things like that against somebody in court.

I recommended that they insert a provision allowing Parliament to set up special courts on specific subjects. For one, I thought they needed a court to decide lawsuits brought by contractors against the government. The government had considerable leverage over road builders, for example, who needed a forum of justice.

I proposed a forum for foreign investors that would increase confidence in investing in Albania. Having a just way to resolve disputes is crucial for anyone considering risking their money in the country. There were judges who liked the idea, but we couldn't get any lawmakers to consider it.

Parliament formally approved the Constitution in 1998. I gave the president a plaque when it passed that was made by my son Wade, with a brass and stainless steel back, and gold letters.

In September 2000, Bob Utter, Charlie Wiggins, and I went to Albania to help resolve the issue of how to decide which cases go to the Supreme Court and which go to the Constitutional Court, and when. The Constitutional Court was led by a judge who had mentored the current Supreme Court chief justice, Thimio Kondi. The Constitutional Court chief introduced Thimio to his future wife, so there was a lot of loyalty between them.

The Utters were picked up from the airport by Thimio's driver, who we dubbed "Michael Schumacher," after the German Formula 1 racer. Like many Albanian drivers at the time, he seemed to have only two gears: park and warp speed. With Bob and Betty in the back seat, he tore out of the airport's dirt parking lot with his siren blaring, reaching speeds at times that felt an awful lot like 100 miles per hour on the chuckhole-infested road from Tirana to the airport.

During the communist era, only the government was allowed to own cars, meaning many drivers in the new Albania were undergoing a steep learning curve. As were pedestrians. The road from the airport to Tirana seemed to have more horse-drawn carts than automobiles. Signage was treated as mere suggestions, and drivers regularly startled pedestrians who had grown up with no concept of "traffic."

I urged "Mr. Schumacher" to go slower when Justice Utter was with us.

Negotiations between the Constitutional Court and the Supreme Court went on for a week. The two courts didn't come to a full agreement, and it took years to work out the differences. A trial court now makes a finding on whether or not it can go forward without a constitutional ruling.

The question was how to determine when to stop a trial and send the case to the Constitutional Court. Everybody knew that if you delayed a case, it could send a message that the case could be resolved through bribery.

A major issue at the time that needed to be addressed was the underfunding of judges, which made curbing bribery and corruption all the more difficult.

I pointed out that in the United States, we have discrimination suits to challenge the underfunding of education. A big part of getting rid of discrimination was to make sure schools were properly funded. The NAACP brought cases against legislatures. One of my roommates, my best friend and best man in my wedding, was lead counsel on many of those cases.

I proposed having the Judges Association bring a lawsuit against the government for not funding the judiciary. That went over like a lead balloon.

'DO YOU KNOW HOW TO GET A HOLD OF ZEF?'

In 2000, a professor at the University of Washington contacted Bob Utter.

"I've got six Albanian professors who have come here for a month. Can you entertain them for a weekend?"

Bob invited Katoo and me to join them at the Utters' home in Olympia. We greeted the professors at the door, and they handed me their business cards before sitting down in the living room to chat. I looked at the card of one of the professors and pointed out that she had the same position Zef Brozi once had at the University of Tirana, professor of criminal procedure law.

"Do you know how to get a hold of Zef?" she asked.

Later, a couple of the professors came into the kitchen while Katoo was there. They looked very agitated, and although they were speaking Albanian, Katoo understood them to be talking about Zef.

Katoo found me and suggested I not bring up Zef's name anymore. I didn't know it at the time, but long after the visit I discovered that this tall lady was the daughter of Sali Berisha, Argita Malltezi.

We invited the Albanian professors to come to Poulsbo the next weekend and have dinner at our home.

We took them to the local Viking Fest, where they seemed to have a good time. One won a giant stuffed animal for knocking over bottles. But after saying goodbye at the ferry dock, it was clear that we never really connected with them. Most of the group was cool toward us and we had never experienced that. We put them back on the ferry and went home scratching our heads.

On a flight to Albania sometime later, I sat across the aisle from an official from the US Embassy in Tirana. Knowing I was from the Seattle area, she mentioned that she had arranged a stay for Albanian professors there.

I began describing my time with them.

"Oh, you're the one they went to the Viking Fest with," she said.

"Yes," I replied.

I didn't know how to react to the fact that she knew about me. But I told her that we never broke the ice with those people.

She nodded. The group had had trouble everywhere they stopped in the US. The US Embassy wasn't aware at the time that Berisha's daughter, using her married name, was on the trip.

It all became clear why we didn't connect.

Argita has become successful in her own right as a lawyer. Opposition parties accused her of acting as a gatekeeper to her father and making money off his name and connections.

A few months after her father was elected prime minister in 2005 on an anti-corruption platform he dubbed "clean hands," she returned home from Pristina, the capital of Kosovo. In Pristina, she had a well-paid position with the United Nations Interim Mission in Kosovo. Once in Tirana, she established three legal firms with one of her friends and co-workers at the UN, Flutura Kola. Within months, they became the go-to solicitors for multinationals looking to invest in Albania's fast-growing economy.

But former clients claim that they employed Malltezi for her family links and to sidestep threats of racketeering, not just for her legal skills.[34] She has denied any wrongdoing, insisting that she never used her father's position to further her career.

On my next trip to Tirana, I called her.

"I want you to know I was very insensitive when you came to our home. I didn't know you were the daughter of Sali Berisha," I said.

"Well, we just assumed that any American who comes to Albania knows who they were talking to and who they were relating with," she replied.

"That's why everybody buys you raki," she continued, "because your file says you like raki."

The famously hospitable Albanians come prepared when they work with foreigners. And, at least when it came to catering to the preferences of their guests, the dossiers the government kept on visitors were useful. But I had lied when I said I liked raki. I said it because it's the national drink. Unfortunately, I also said I liked lamb brains.

We actually are still in contact with several of the professors who were on the Seattle trip. One became a member of Parliament, another a Constitutional Court judge, and another a judge on the European Court of Human Rights.

Members of the Albanian Supreme Court came several times to the US, including visits to Poulsbo, where they would stay in homes. Katoo oversaw making sure they were happy. And I made them work.

On one occasion, we had planned a visit to Perkins Coie, the largest law firm in Seattle. Attorneys at the prestigious firm were going to show the Albanian judges how they prepared a case for appellate hearings.

We started off with a visit to the Boeing Museum of Flight, south of Seattle's downtown. As we prepared to head to the downtown offices of Perkins Coie, Justice Petrit Plloci, speaking for the court, approached me.

"Roger, you are working us too hard. We need to go back to your house and rest," he said.

The justices made it clear that they weren't willing to go on. So, with embarrassment, I had to make a phone call and back out of the Perkins Coie meeting.

When we got back to my home in Poulsbo, I discovered their true intent. With haste, they gathered in front of my TV in the basement to watch a big match in soccer's World Cup.

FREEDOM HANGING ON A CHAD

Albania now had a constitution that spelled out how to conduct elections. The issue then was how to ensure that the final vote count actually represented the will of the people.

In 2001, on the heels of America's contentious "hanging chad" presidential election, I received a call from the president of the Constitutional Court, Fehmi Abdiu, asking if we would host a seminar on constitutional election laws.

An election was coming up that summer for Parliament, which has the authority to choose the president.

"Roger, we want you to do a seminar to train our case workers on managing the election. We've got a system of appeal. The Constitutional

Court must hear every claim of improper registration within ten days," Abdiu said. «So we've got to be prepared."

I told him I didn't know anything about voting laws and rights.

"But you know how to get people. You always bring over interesting people," he said

"I'll see what I can do," I replied in a moment of weakness.

I called Sam Ericsson in Washington, DC.

"You know, Roger," he said. "There's a lawyer from Minneapolis. His first name is Roger, and his last name, I think, is Swedish. I saw him on TV, representing the Florida legislature in Bush v. Gore."

I had come to know a federal judge in Minneapolis named Paul Magnuson through his frequent visits to Albania. Paul first came to Albania in the late '90s at the request of then-Supreme Court Chief Justice Thimio Kondi. I called Paul and asked him if he knew of the Roger who was in the Bush case.

"His name is Roger Magnusson," Paul replied.

"Is he your brother?" I asked.

"He's not my biological brother, but he's my spiritual brother," Paul said.

Paul had a plaque on the wall of his office with the words of Micah 6:8: "What does the Lord require of you but to do justice, and to love kindness, and to walk humbly with your God?"

Roger Magnuson was at the center of the Bush v. Gore case in 2000, in which the US presidential election was decided by a mere six hundred votes.[35] And he argued before the Minnesota state Supreme Court on behalf of Sen. Norm Coleman in the Republican lawmaker's case against challenger Al Franken in the 2008 election.

Magnuson earned a juris doctorate in 1971 from Harvard University Law School, where he was a member of the board of editors of the Harvard Law Review and an officer of the Harvard Corp. After law school, he studied as a Knox fellow for a year at Magdalen College at Oxford University in England, receiving a Bachelor of Civil Law degree.

I called Roger Magnuson.

We talked about his role in the disputed 2000 presidential election, representing the Florida State Senate.

"I know it's late notice," I said, "but could you possibly come?"

Magnuson said he had a case in London that would have to settle for him to make it.

"And that's not going to happen. I'm going to be tied up all that week, getting ready for trial," Magnuson said.

Well, it was worth a try, I thought.

A short time later, the phone rang, and it was a judge from Florida.

"Hello, this is Judge John Kuder."

Kuder was senior chief judge of the First Judicial Circuit Court in Florida during the Bush vs. Gore recount.

"I saw your website," he said, referring to Advocates International. Kuder explained that he was intrigued by the opportunity of helping judges in former communist countries.

"Is there anything for me to do?

The London case settled, and we had Roger Magnuson, a key legal figure in one of the most contentious presidential elections in US history, and Florida judge John Kuder.

They presented seminars in Tirana on election laws and managing elections. And as an added treat, they gave us all the skinny on how Bush won.

Kuder told the Albanian judges that it was because America's rule of law could handle a contested election that war didn't erupt and there weren't tanks in the streets.

My youngest son, Toby, came along on that trip after graduating from Washington State University. Toby was pursuing a career in architectural design, and before arriving in Albania, we took a tour of modern architecture in northern Italy.

He wanted to go see some of the things we had done in Albania, so he shadowed us. On our last night, the president invited us for dinner, along with Kuder and Magnuson.

We had tickets for a show at the amphitheater in Tirana, which was built by the Soviet Union. There were as many as five thousand people. I didn't know what the main act would be ahead of time. It turned out to be the US Army glee club.

I had taken Toby to our Army battle positions in Germany on a previous trip.

"Dad, this is amazing," he said. "You started off your career here in Europe, defending the US against the Soviet Union for the invasion we thought was sure to come," he said. "And you're completing your career here in Albania, with the Soviet Union now history."

'HOW FAR YOU HAVE COME'

We had planned for a Constitutional Court seminar in May 2002, but it was canceled for some reason. Instead, there was a Day of Justice event to celebrate the court's tenth anniversary.

On our first night, we had dinner with the Supreme Court chief justice, Thimio Kondi, and the former speaker of Parliament, Pjetër Arbnori. It was Pjetër, who ten years earlier had told us that Parliament members didn't know how to get along with each other and needed rules.

As I sat in Thimio's office, I thought "how far you have come." In that office a decade earlier, the chief justice at the time said the greatest need the court had was for paper on which to record their decisions.

I was given a big book with all the written decisions from 2000 and 2001. No other post-communist country, that we knew of, was doing this kind of documentation at the time.

We then were scheduled to have coffee with Abdiu, the president of the Constitutional Court. Two years earlier, Bob Utter and I had been called in to mediate between Abdiu and Kondi, who were refusing to speak with each other. Now, they may not have been the best of friends, but they were cordial and working with each other.

"I have the rest of the court assembled, I would like for you to address them," Abdiu told me.

I had not prepared anything, so I said, "Lord, you're going to have to pull it all together for me here."

Before the Constitutional Court seminar was canceled, I had in mind addressing religious liberty, so I decided to ad lib.

We passed out the "Justice is Truth in Action" paperweights, and after commending the court for how far it had come in ten years, explained the connection between truth and justice.

"Some would say there is no truth or that each person must find his own truth. Nothing could be more wrong," I said. "There is truth, and it is our duty to seek the truth in each case and in each issue that comes before you. If you do this, you will build a growing credibility and acceptance with the citizens of Albania."

I recounted my trip the previous day to the city of Shkodra, north of Tirana. There, in November 1990, Catholics and Muslims helped each other restore the places of worship that had been destroyed during the communist era.

I noted the religious strife in the former Yugoslavia, some fifty miles away, that certainly was in the minds of the drafters of the Constitution in 1997 and 1998.

"Your Constitution has excellent religious freedom provisions," I said. "In fact, they may be the best in the world."

I said I believed that religious freedom is the most important freedom, encompassing the freedoms of speech, conscience, and assembly.

"Look around the world," I said. "Those nations that deny religious liberty also deny other basic freedoms."

I also drew a connection between religious freedom and economic prosperity, arguing that the liberties supported by religious freedom make possible the marketplace of ideas on which free enterprise thrives.

Thimio had asked me to speak at the Day of Justice ceremony that evening, and I focused on the court's remarkable progress over the past decade.

After the ceremony, a law professor who was one of the first we worked with, Alex Luarasi, came up to me.

"Thank you for reminding us how far we have come. We get so involved in the strife that we forget the progress we have made," he said.

THE UBIQUITOUS BUNKERS

Albania's president at the time was Alfred Moisiu. We both served in the army, which gave us a personal connection.

Nicknamed "the father of bunkers," Moisiu, a general, was appointed by Enver Hoxha to oversee the construction and installation of hundreds of thousands of bunkers throughout Albania from 1975 to 1982.

Moisiu estimates that as many as five hundred thousand were built. Factories ran twenty-four hours a day, seven days a week to churn them out. In a country that struggled to feed and house its people, the financial burden was considerable, with each costing the equivalent of a two-bedroom apartment.

The dictator Hoxha insisted the bunkers were necessary for Albania's survival, claiming that the "anti-Marxist" communist Yugoslav dictator Josip Broz Tito was plotting to seize Albania and turn it into Yugoslavia's seventh republic. On top of that, Hoxha warned his people, US Marines and NATO allies were prepared to hit Albania's beaches.

The mushroom-like concrete bunkers, reinforced with thirteen layers of steel, were installed not only on beaches but in cities, on mountaintops, and in remote rural areas. Hoxha also ordered the army to place spikes on stakes in thousands of vineyards to impale airborne troops.

Kujtim Çashku, an award-winning Albanian film director and screenwriter, has characterized the bunkers as "a symbol of totalitarianism," representing Hoxha's "isolation psychology" and siege mentality, which were intended to unite the people against a perceived common enemy.[36]

Hoxha executed critics of the project, including a defense minister who also was a member of the Politburo, Gen. Beqir Balluku. In a 1974 speech, the general disputed Hoxha's contention that Albania was threatened equally by both the United States and the Soviet Union. One of the chief bunker designers, Josif Zagali, was imprisoned by Hoxha during a purge in 1974 on false charges of "sabotage" as a "foreign agent."

After the fall of the communist regime in 1991, the bunkers did serve as a temporary home to Albanians who suffered from the severe housing shortage. Others were turned into cafes.

Moisiu asked me about my experience in Vietnam, and we talked about the issue of fear, in politics and warfare.

I said fear can be paralyzing and lead to all kinds of bad decisions, but sometimes can be valuable.

"Don't let fear drive you away. Listen to what your fears are," I said.

"What do you mean?" Moisiu asked.

I recalled the assessment I made one day on the battlefield in Vietnam that I needed to take a hill.

"I asked the Lord for wisdom. It turned out to be the right choice," I said.

During the Vietnam War, the Albanian Armed Forces sent at least one small group of reconnaissance officers to Vietnam for training under China's communist regime, according to Albanian Brigadier-General Perlat Sula.[37] At that time, China was assisting the People's Army of Vietnam.

In 2005, Moisiu surprised me—as well as Paul Magnuson and John Walker—by awarding each of us a special presidential medal. I regarded it as a way of honoring the many attorneys, judges, and legal scholars from all over the world who had come to serve over the previous decade and a half.

Before the ceremony, we were alone in an ante room. As we prepared to enter a conference room, where dignitaries and media were gathered, Moisiu paused.

"Roger, you might want to zip up your fly. We'll be taking pictures."

I replied, "You'd better check yours, too, Mr. President."

The English inscription of the plaque he gave me, alongside the Albanian, read:

The Medal "For Special Civil Merits"

"For the notable contribution of many years, for the tireless and dedicated work in assisting the Albanian Judiciary to get it closer to the rule of law standards.

For introducing to Albania, the best practices and expertise of the functioning of the judicial system in the United States.

Tirana, on December 05, 2005

Number 4713

THE PRESIDENT

ALFRED MOISIU

I AM SHEFFIELD

Later that year, we found out that my status in Albania, and Europe for that matter, was more complex.

We rented a car at the airport in Venice, Italy, to drive to an Advocates International conference in Rijeka, Croatia, via the neighboring former Yugoslav republic of Slovenia. The border guard at the Slovenian border took our passports and was on the phone for a long time. He finally handed back our passports, with a slip of paper inside mine that contained a message in Slovenian. He turned us away, declaring we would not be allowed in the country. The car papers were not in order, he claimed, and we would have to return to Venice.

Believing the rental car was the issue, we started back to the Venice airport. We spent the night near the airport. The next day we went back to the rental car desk. They said the paperwork was in order. So we decided we would try a different border crossing. To our amazement, on the autostrada heading toward Trieste we found ourselves passing Sam and Jill Casey, who also were headed to the conference.

Sam Casey succeeded Sam Ericsson as CEO of the Christian Legal Society and then became executive vice president and general counsel of Advocates International.

We linked up with the Caseys, and we decided to try a different, less traveled border crossing. But they turned us away again. We had no other choice but to return the rental car. We were able to turn it in in the border town of Trieste, Italy. At the rental car office, I showed the agent the piece of paper, and he translated it.

It said that I was declared a danger to the European Union and not permitted to enter Slovenia.

We decided to take a bus to Rijeka. The bus had to travel through a sliver of Slovenia to get to Croatia. The border guard came aboard the bus. Starting at the back, he thoroughly examined every passport. Katoo and I were at the front of the bus, sweating bullets. We prayed that he would not come to the last page of my jumbo-sized passport—it had an extra 32 pages—where he would find the stamp denying entrance to Slovenia.

The guard went through 63 pages of my passport and handed it back to me without looking at the last page.

To this day, I don't know why I was flagged.

In Albania, I was told my file included a statement that I had been trained as a spy at West Point.

I later learned more.

The US had given some technical equipment and support to the Albanian secret police so they could monitor phone calls. Shortly after that, I was working on organizing a conference with Turi Metani, the legal adviser to President Bamir Topi. I got a call in my office in Poulsbo from Turi's cell phone. But it wasn't Turi. A very deep voice came on the line.

"Who is this?" the man said.

"Who is *this?*" I asked.

"I am Sheffield."

He finally hung up. I then phoned John Withers, the US ambassador to Albania.

"I just got a call from Turi's cell phone," I said. "Didn't we give the

Albanians a listening device on the condition that they wouldn't use it on their own people?

"Yes," he replied.

"Well, somebody has Turi's phone. They're listening to the president's office. And I'm concerned for Turi, because he's been helping us."

John called me back thirty minutes later.

"Your friend is OK, but the listening device is not," he said.

It turned out, as I learned through some of my friends in Tirana, that the Albanians had identified me by the code name Sheffield.

The US didn't want to create any problems for Albania, so the incident was not reported.

DIPLOMATIC PROTOCOL

Withers was appointed US ambassador to Albania in August 2007. Prior to Withers' appointment, John Walker Jr.—the cousin of President George W. Bush—made a pitch for me to become ambassador.

Walker arranged a meeting for me at the White House with President Bush.

On the morning of the day the meeting was scheduled, however, the State Department announced Withers, a career diplomat, had been appointed to the position. Everybody was tripping over themselves at the White House, because I had flown to DC for that meeting.

But Katoo and I became instant friends with Withers, an African American whose father was a member of the famous Buffalo Soldiers. Withers, who earned a BA in history from Harvard and a PhD in modern Chinese history from Yale, was surprisingly familiar with a significant chapter in Katoo's family history. Katoo, seated next to him at lunch at the ambassador's residence, told him that her grandfather and great grandfather served in the Chinese Maritime Customs Service under Sir Robert Hart. Withers had studied in China and was familiar with Hart's crucial role in saving China from collapse, helping equalize trade between China and Europe.

At the time, Berisha and his Democratic Party had regained power after making a remarkable comeback in 2005 following the collapse of the government in 1997 under his leadership. Berisha was now prime minister, which according to the new constitution, made him the head of state, with more power than the presidency.

I was having difficulty persuading the US government that they should not trust Berisha. In fact, it took an entire car trip with John Walker to Pogradec to convince him of that fact. He had been briefed by somebody at the State Department that he shouldn't listen to the criticism. Diplomats were arguing that there were people out to get Berisha for personal reasons.

Ultimately, it became clear that the problem was that the US had a policy it didn't want interrupted by the facts on the ground. I wish I had a hundred dollars for every time I heard an official say we can't interfere with the internal politics of a sovereign nation.

We decided to develop a protocol for Berisha, as prime minister, and the president to sign, pledging their active support for an independent and just judiciary.

The "Protocol for the Judiciary" read as follows:

Whereas the Albanian Judiciary is an essential institution of Albania;

Whereas a credible and effective judiciary is a key factor for the growth and development of Albania;

And,

Whereas the leaders of all branches of the Albanian government wish to support and advance the development of the Judiciary.

NOW, THEREFORE THE UNDERSIGNED LEADERS solemnly covenant, pledge, and agree as follows:

1. They do and will support the development of a credible and effective judiciary in Albania.

2. They will promptly report to the Inspectorate of the High Council of Justice, or other appropriate authorities, allegations of corruption of specific judicial officials, advocates or others who seek to corrupt the judicial process.

3. They will not engage in conduct or activity which denigrates the Judiciary, except to report investigations of specific acts of improper conduct.

4. They lend their full support to the prosecution of judicial officers, lawyers, litigants, and others who attempt to corrupt any judicial official, to the fullest extent of the law.

5. They will encourage others to support this protocol.

I showed it to Withers.

"This is great," he said, "it confronts the main problems."

We took Withers on a tour of the courthouse in Tirana, near the pyramid on the north side of the river, which at the time was always full of garbage. The court had nine courtrooms for more than sixty judges. I reminded the ambassador that the paltry pay that judges were receiving only exacerbated the culture of bribery.

In a 2008 meeting with Berisha and President Topi, I presented them with my concerns about the judiciary. I asked Berisha to sign the protocol.

Berisha had promised to sign it when Albania became a member of NATO. But when Albania finally became a member in 2009, he still refused.

When President George W. Bush went to Albania in the summer of 2007, the White House ignored my advice to reach out to Moisiu. I argued he stood for an independent judiciary.

In one meeting with Berisha, I asked him if he believed in God and thought there might be divine providence in his return to power.

"Do you think maybe he's giving you another chance to get it right?" I asked.

"Could be," he said.

The meeting ended shortly after that.

Many years later I discovered that Berisha had hired Tom Ridge, the first Department of Homeland Security director, in September 2006 as a consultant for $480,000 per year.[38] Ridge's main tasks were to boost Albania's NATO bid and Berisha's relationship with the US government.

Apparently Berisha convinced Ridge he was a true advocate for democracy. As I look back, none of my advice was considered by Washington while Ridge was employed by Berisha.

I specifically advised the White House to have President Bush greet Moisiu, the titular head of state, during the 2007 visit to Albania. But Berisha kept Moisiu far away from Bush.

TIMELESS PRINCIPLES

On October 23, 2009, we held a "Conference on Integrity" that was focused on addressing corruption.

I recited "timeless principles" that address integrity and corruption, found in the Bible, beginning with the Golden Rule, treating others the way you want to be treated, as the "foundation for equal justice under the law":

"A good name is more valuable than silver or gold."

"It is not good to be partial to the wicked or deprive the innocent of justice."

"When the good people triumph there is great elation; but when the wicked rise to power, men go into hiding."

"Overcome evil with good."

Fear is a normal human emotion, I said, but we must not be controlled by it.

"Fear of reprisals, harm, attacks on family, smears in the media, harm to reputation, planting false reports and not having the garbage picked up" are common in Albanian life, I said.

I recalled the admonition to overcome fear with good and quoted Deuteronomy 31:6:

> Be strong and courageous. Do not be terrified because of them, for the
> Lord your God goes with you; he will never leave you nor forsake you.

In God's charge to Joshua, in the first chapter of the book of Joshua, "Be strong and courageous" is repeated three times.

I recalled—at a time when it looked like this whole endeavor might never work—being uplifted by the refrain as it was repeated over and over by the choir at my Poulsbo church.

> Be strong and take courage
>
> Do not fear or be dismayed
>
> For the Lord will go before you
>
> And His light will show the way

12

THE DIFFICULT TRUTH

ON ONE OF HIS MANY FLIGHTS TO TIRANA, Sam Ericsson was reading a book in which his attention was drawn to a quote by nineteenth-century British reform prime minister Benjamin Disraeli, "I say justice is truth in action."

Sam was scheduled to speak that night at a dinner with Albanian judges, and the phrase fit perfectly with his opening remarks.

The speech must have made an impression. Shortly after that, I received a Christmas card from Thimio Kondi with a header, in both English and Albanian, that said "justice is truth in action."

The Albanian Supreme Court then adopted the phrase as their motto. It's inscribed on the wall that leads to the staircase up to the main hearing room at the Supreme Court. My graphic designer son, Wade, created paperweights featuring the motto, and we brought ninety of them to distribute to judges.

The slogan "justice is truth in action" is believed to have been coined by the acclaimed French thinker Joseph Joubert, a Christian moralist and essayist who served briefly as a justice of the peace from 1790 to 1792.[39] The idea is also expressed in the iconic symbol of justice, the crusading, blindfolded woman with a scale in one hand and a sword in the other. The English essayist and poet Joseph Addison explained the symbol this way: "Justice discards party, friendship, kindred and is, therefore, represented as blind. It signifies that it is impartial and is devoid of prejudice. She bears no ill-will to one or the other and favors neither."[40]

That was the noble aim for Albania shared by many of its jurists, but as I drafted a speech while on a plane trip to Tirana in 2010, I could not avoid addressing the public's "lack of confidence in the Albanian judiciary."

"I hear the complaints of citizens," I wrote, and "the difficult truth" is that "many in the judiciary want to end the corruption but are afraid to act."

"A strong and independent judiciary is a cornerstone of democracy," I pointed out. And it's "time to overcome your fears and discouragement and no longer tolerate corruption."

"Until you commit to this you will not find progress."

I threw away the draft.

I once again recalled my conversation with Father Zef Pllumi about overcoming evil with good and his experience with the abusive guard whose life he had saved. We needed some Father Zefs in the judiciary and in the other branches of government to put aside their fears, resentments, old scores, and personal ambitions, and stand up for what is good and right.

I got involved in an Albanian legal case in which a contractor who had finished a project was suing the Ministry of Transportation for not paying him. A state employee who had the evidence to support the contractor's case was weighing whether or not to testify against a top official.

Here was a possible breakthrough case that could serve as a legal precedent as well as an inspiration for the whole nation.

I met with the state employee at an inconspicuous place at the back of an outdoor restaurant, occasionally scanning the scene as we talked to make sure no one was eavesdropping. She told me she was being pressured not to testify.

"If I have to testify against him, he will probably go to jail," she said of the official.

I told her I would look into her options, and I asked her to meet me for breakfast. I was fairly certain she could get immunity for anything she had done wrong. I talked to the president's legal adviser, and he said they could take care of the pardon. I never disclosed who she was or any facts that would expose her.

She met me the next morning but said she would not stay for breakfast.

"I can't do this," she said.

"Why not?"

"When I was coming in this morning to the hotel, there was a lady out sweeping the sidewalk. The last time I had seen her was when she was in the second grade, when she turned in her family for listening to Radio Free Europe. Her family was in prison for the rest of her growing-up years. She stayed with aunts and uncles. She never showed up again in school," the state employee explained.

"I can't do this to this family. It would destroy their lives."

Even though Albania is no longer under communist rule, "we have to be careful in this transition period," she explained.

She walked off. I walked off. What could I say to her?

She was overcome by emotion when she saw that woman. I don't know whether or not she was a weak person. But her reaction was not unlike Thimio's reply to me when I reminded him that when good men don't act, evil prevails.

A FREE PEOPLE

Corruption was the main complaint in many phone calls I had with judges.

A woman on the Constitutional Court called me out of the blue saying she would resign because she was getting calls telling her how to decide a case. Her children were being threatened.

As similar complaints emerged, we tried to establish a committee of judges to report the threats and corruption, but it never materialized. If such a panel had been formed, it would have to overcome the perception by the average Albanian that every judge was on the take.

There needed to be some way to ensure that the judges who are appointed to hold people accountable for their actions are themselves held accountable.

During his famous tour of America in 1831, French diplomat and political philosopher Alexis de Tocqueville observed that the American experiment of governance by the people relied on citizens with an internal moral compass. The more its people governed their personal actions, the less government was needed to ensure a just, free, and prosperous society.

In *Democracy in America*,[41] Tocqueville argued a free society requires a religious foundation. Nearly every human action, he said, tends to "arise from a very general idea men have conceived of God, of his relations with the human race, of the nature of their souls, and of their duties towards those like them."

People can safely govern, he argued, if they believe they will be held accountable for their use of power. "What makes a people master of itself, if it has not submitted to God?" he asked.

Tocqueville was a great-grandson of a famed French statesman, Malesherbes, who was a campaigner for the rights of French Protestants and Jews just before the French Revolution.[42] He was an advocate for freedom of the press, arguing the nation can find truth only through free discourse. In the trial of King Louis XVI in 1792, Malesherbes was appointed, at his own request, a defender of the monarch. Although he had been a critic of royal abuses, he was arrested soon after his legal advocacy for the king and guillotined as a royalist, along with his daughter and grandchildren.

The German anti-Nazi theologian and pastor Dietrich Bonhoeffer observed a fundamental difference between the French and American revolutions. The United States, he said, had a federal constitution that took into account the concept of original sin. Consequently, the American republic "is not founded upon the emancipated man but, quite on the contrary, upon the kingdom of God and the limitation of all earthly powers by the sovereignty of God."[43]

THE HEART OF THE MATTER

Many of the Albanian judges have had the opportunity to experience American life, staying with our church families in Poulsbo and other places we visit in the United States. In the early days of their new democracy, our Albanian friends were stunned by the things they saw on their visits to the United States. The abundantly supplied grocery stores with a mind-boggling variety of choices. The homes that could easily accommodate multiple Albanian families. The order. But it was their exposure to the grassroots, entering the homes of American families, that had the greatest impact.

They often have told us that being with families, mostly from our church, nourished their souls. Shpresa Becaj, who eventually became chief justice of the Supreme Court, was among those who was deeply impacted.

When they would stay in our homes, they sometimes would choose to go to church with us. And in our many, often animated, interactions, we would share with them our love for Jesus and our belief that he is the source of life and the motivation for all that we do. Many expressed much joy when they were with us, allowing us to see the beauty of their souls.

There was also an underlying desperation for their children's futures. Regularly, we would be asked to help a son or daughter come to America for schooling.

On one occasion, Judge Agim Gjoleka traveled to Poulsbo for eye surgery. I remember driving back home with him from the clinic along spectacular Liberty Bay. With the sun shining on the snow-capped

Olympic Mountains, I smiled as I thought to myself that Agim was seeing that for the first time.

THE TABLE HAS BEEN SET

At a conference we helped host in Tirana in December 2011, I finally was ready to talk about "the difficult truth." The event was titled "Current Reality in Albania and its Future Constitutional and Legal Challenges."

"The difficult truth," I said, is that there is "public distrust" in a judiciary many saw as "lacking independence and subject to improper influence from other branches of government and individuals who seek to weaken its independence even further."

But I urged Albanians to learn from the mistakes and experiences of the United States and others, and consider the principle of the separation of powers, which has developed over two millennia.

The "beautiful system" of separating legislative, executive, and judicial powers, as the eighteenth-century French philosopher Montesquieu called it, offered the best protection from tyranny, preserving individual rights.

I offered eight recommendations, specific reforms that if adopted, "would lay the foundation for a highly effective judiciary."

They included a constitutional amendment requiring the Assembly to provide sufficient funding for the judiciary and adopt laws and protocols prohibiting undue influence on judicial decisions, including "prohibiting political leaders from communicating with judges about assigned cases."

"It is within the grasp of Albania to have a strong, effective, and independent judiciary," I told the judges. "The table that speaker Arbnori mentioned has been set. Albanians have enjoyed the fruits for twenty years.

"You know now what to eat and when to eat it. You know now what needs to be done. You do have an excellent constitution, although it may still need 'adjustments.'

"If you fail to act, the banquet may come to an end, and the food and fruits of liberty may spoil. But if you act to preserve for the future these hard-won fruits, then you and your children and grandchildren will thrive for generations to come."

Six months later, in May 2012, I was a moderator at the conference for chief justices of the Central and Eastern European nations that were transitioning from authoritarian rule.

In a talk titled "Practical Ideas to Respond to Corruption," I cited a confidential survey that Advocates International had conducted of attorneys and judges from 108 countries. They were asked to identify the greatest hindrance to justice in their nation. Corruption was number one.

I offered five principles to consider when responding to corruption:

A good name is more valuable than silver or gold.

Overcome evil with good. Overcome fear and discouragement with courage and strength

Partiality and corruption adversely impact the independence of the judiciary.

Treat others the way you want to be treated.

When the wicked prevail, people fear and go into hiding but when the good triumph there is great elation.

We always tried to combine principles with practical methods. And two were developed from the results of the Advocates survey:

When presented with a threat or offer of corruption, repeat the offer in different words, "Are you saying x?"

Establish a policy that a judge may withdraw from a case when a bribe has been offered or a threat made.

THE ULTIMATE FOUNDATION

In June 2012, we celebrated the twentieth anniversary of the Constitutional Court. I delivered a speech on the crucial role of the court to protect the freedoms guaranteed by the constitution.

I felt it was time to be bolder and talk more about the Judeo-Christian foundation of the US legal system.

The principle for which America's Founders pledged their lives, fortunes, and sacred honor, I pointed out, was the "unalienable rights" that are "endowed by their creator."

"When we deny this source, then the conclusion that these rights come from governments, or parliaments or wise and strong leaders cannot be avoided," I said.

And that conclusion, as history shows, ultimately leads to tyranny.

"When the people accept this rationale then these putative philosopher-kings, as Plato designated them, rationalize the need to take away those rights for 'the good of the people,'" I told the attendees celebrating the Constitutional Court's first two decades.

I cited the line in Dostoyevsky's *The Brothers Karamazov*, that if there is no God, "everything is permitted."

"The dictators of the twentieth century and their tragic and horrific actions are a legacy of these warnings."

I pointed to the virtues I saw in the Albanian people, their extraordinary hospitality and care for others rooted in their ancient *Code of Leke Dukagjini*, particularly in the concept of *besa*.

I recalled one of the many instances in which I was the beneficiary of besa.

I had dinner with a friend and his wife at the Piazza restaurant near Skanderbeg Square that lasted until midnight. My friend had no vehicle, and we were unable to find a taxi. He and his wife insisted on walking with me to my hotel, which was perhaps more than a kilometer away. Then they had to walk more than twice that distance back to their apartment. He explained that besa required him to ensure that I arrived at the hotel safely.

"Albanians genuinely care for family and close friends," I said. "Relationships are important and valued. This emphasis is conducive to strong families, the building block of society."

I urged the members of the court to interpret the constitution in light of the preamble, "with responsibility for the future, and with faith in God and other universal values."

I recalled the words of an elderly Albanian trial court judge who had suffered under the communist regime.

"The law is my friend," he told me.

I asked the Albanian judges and dignitaries: "Is the law your friend? If it is, then treat it like one, follow besa and deliver your friend to the next generation, safe and sound."

To do this will take strength, courage, and persistence, I emphasized.

"If you do, the words of your constitution will become meaningful, Albania will prosper, and its people will enjoy the blessings of liberty."

BREAKING FROM TYRANNY

I returned to Tirana in December 2012, when two former presidents and former chief justice Thimio Kondi convened a conference to consider revisions of the constitution adopted in 1998.

Several ambassadors were asked to review the revisions. I was asked to speak on judicial reform. Eventually, the constitution was amended to restrict the immunity of top public officials, politicians, and judges. Other amendments expanded the scope of public officials required by law to disclose their assets. And stricter sanctions were imposed for violations of conflict-of-interest provisions.

However, in a 2014 report[44], the global watchdog Transparency International ranked Albania as one of the most corrupt countries in Europe. Further, Albania was ranked as the European country in which the highest proportion of companies expect they will be forced to give a "gift" to secure a public contract.

Citizens typically were confronted with bribery when accessing public services, according to Transparency International's 2013 "Global

Corruption Barometer."[45] And the judiciary (81 percent) was the service most susceptible to bribes, followed by health (80 percent), education (70 percent), police (58 percent), and civil services (52 percent).

Significantly, Transparency International recognized "recent progress on the legal front," but only 10 percent of Albanians surveyed believed that corruption had decreased in the previous two years. And 96 percent believed corruption in the public sector remained a problem.

BREAKING FROM THE PAST

During a judicial conference in 2014, President Bujar Nishani invited Katoo and me to a private meeting with him and the chief justice.

It was Katoo he wanted to hear from.

Nishani had been in the room at the conference when US federal court Judge Paul Magnuson noted in his remarks a conversation he had had with Katoo. She had suggested that Albanians teach principles of democracy in their schools. Katoo didn't know Paul was going to quote her to the whole group.

But it caught Nishani's attention, and he invited us out to lunch for a personal discussion. He took us to the Sofra e Ariut restaurant, where we were given a table in the private Laura Bush salon, as it was dubbed after the then-first lady dined there in 2007.

It was Katoo and me, the president, and a translator.

Katoo explained the rationale: From the grassroots to the pinnacles of power, she said, Albanians had little knowledge of how a democratic society functions.

"Unless the people understand democracy, there will never be any social cohesion," she said. "There will never be a break from their tyrannical past."

The idea came to her, she said, during our visit a few days before to Shkodra, where we joined the mayor and religious leaders in a discussion about how Catholics and Muslims had helped each other restore their places of worship.

One of the participants, a Catholic, asked us to meet with him the next day. During the conversation, Zef Brozi's name came up.

His countenance immediately changed.

"Zef Brozi is a criminal!" he said. "He needs to be put in jail and executed. He's killed more people than Hoxha."

After her initial shock and confusion, Katoo later said it dawned on her that ordinary citizens had no clue why Zef stood up to Berisha. They were the victims of the propaganda machine meant to keep Berisha in power. She recounted to this man the overwhelming evidence of Berisha's corruption and his control of the public narrative.

"My husband had the actual printout of the vote in Parliament to remove Zef, showing that it was falsified," she said.

"We had proof that Berisha was lying," Katoo continued. "And the US State Department believed Zef and helped him escape Albania."

But the mind of this prominent religious and civic leader, this friend of the mayor, was unmoved.

'JUSTICE FOR ALL'

Truth is the absolute foundation for justice. But since becoming an attorney in 1975, I've observed that in the legal profession, truth increasingly has been treated as an obstacle to political or personal objectives, including in the United States.

In fact, Americans' confidence in major US institutions—including the criminal justice system—is at an all-time low, according to a Gallup survey.[46] Some people are charged for crimes, while others, under the same circumstances, are not. And there are prosecutors in major US cities who have refused to adhere to the rule of law, insisting they are following a higher law of "social justice."

The campaigns of many of those district attorneys were financed by George Soros. And the reach of the billionaire activist's judicial "reform" has extended to Albania.

According to documents obtained through a Freedom of Information Act lawsuit by Judicial Watch, $9 million in US taxpayer funds went to a group with links to the Soros Open Society Foundation in Albania to carry out a "Justice for All" campaign.[47] The stated objective of the five-year effort is to increase the public's confidence in Albania's judicial system. With funding from USAID, Open Society-Albania and its experts created the controversial Strategy Document for Albanian Judicial Reform.

The document states that the "overall goal of the reform is to create a justice system that is credible, fair, independent, professional and oriented toward services, open, accountable and efficient; one that will enjoy the confidence of the public, will support the country's sustainable social-economic development and will enable its integration into the European family."

However, the Soros-funded reform effort effectively gave the prime minister and his Socialist Party government control over the judiciary. It has established a strict vetting process with the noble aim of weeding out corrupt judges and prosecutors. But the process has been used by the party in power to remove opponents from office. Consequently, just judges have been eliminated while corrupt jurists have been retained. The government, critics charge, has thus been able to enact laws without checks and balances.

Ironically, with his party out of power, Sali Berisha has become a critic of Soros and of executive branch control of the judicial system.

In an interview with New York Post editor Miranda Devine in February 2022,[48] Berisha said that in the early days after the fall of communism he was grateful for Soros' part in helping Albania create a civil society.

However, Berisha continued, "in a short time, it became crystal clear that he was creating a monastic model of civil society."

"The Soros group dictated everything," Berisha said. "So, we have now a justice system, totally controlled by the government....The heads of judiciary institutions, in violation of constitutional laws, are for the moment former communist prosecutors."

DIVINE COINCIDENCES

To make a case in court, lawyers typically formulate linear, step-by-step, rational arguments built on empirical and circumstantial evidence. We think ahead, like chess players, and try to anticipate the arguments and moves of our opponents. But life seldom unfolds as planned.

As I look back over more than a quarter of a century and more than fifty trips to Albania from Poulsbo, Washington, it's clear that on every journey to that beloved land, and to others on its behalf, the best laid plans took an unforeseen course.

The Washington Post observed in a feature on Sam Ericsson and his global work that the "sovereignty of God is the lens through which he sees a tightly woven tapestry of 'divine coincidences.'"[49] For Ericsson, 'His-story,' or true history, is living life sensitive to the vertical dimension so that 'when God's will and our actions coincide, we have a coincidence.'"

I share Sam's belief that we all are part of something much bigger than ourselves. It has been wondrous and often humbling to see encounters, events, and relationships improbably woven together.

On one of our many journeys across the country, we were reminded of some of the "divine coincidences" we witnessed.

The president of the Constitutional Court, Vladimir Kristo, took Katoo and me on a two-day overnight trip to southeastern Albania, to the towns of Korça and Pogradec. We met at the Constitutional Court in Tirana and rode with Vladimir in his car. When we left Tirana that evening it was dark and pouring rain, with thunder and lightning. We thought it would just be a simple road trip. But we had an entourage of at least two court cars along with police motorcycles on the sides and a squad car trailing.

The lights on the police car flashed the whole time as we were escorted over treacherous mountain passes with no guardrails. As we left a jurisdiction, the police escort would peel off and another would take over. It went that way for the entire five-hour journey.

In Pogradec, by spectacular Lake Ohrid on the border with the country of North Macedonia, we ate at a restaurant with a beautiful garden, ponds, bridges, and weeping willows. The restaurant clearly was well established. We sat at a large corner table, and our hosts insisted that I sit at the head.

They sheepishly told me I was seated where Enver Hoxha would sit, in the very chair he used. It was then that they informed us that we had slept in Hoxha's bed at the villa in Vlore on that Fourth of July nearly two decades earlier.

During the trip to Pogradec, we stopped in Korça, where Albanian hero Gjerasim Qiriazi established a girl's school. We visited the chief judge of the court of appeals there, Majlinda. She proudly pulled from her courtroom closet a robe that we had given her in 1995. It still had the name—"Karen" or a name like that—affixed to the inside of the collar, a remnant of its past life in a choir somewhere in Alabama.

It reminded me of the words of an Albanian Supreme Court justice during a visit to the US Supreme Court hosted by Ruth Bader Ginsburg. After our time at the court, we were at dinner at the Mayflower Hotel, which had once served as the Albanian embassy in Washington.

"Roger, tell us the story of the robes," one judge asked. "There are all kinds of stories flying around Albania about how you got them."

I told how, against all odds, the precise number needed—292—came at literally the last minute, recalling how Jesus multiplied the loaves and the fishes in the feeding of the five thousand.

One of the judges had never heard the story.

"We can't get rid of these robes. They are a gift from God," she said.

In Korça, on the courtroom wall, was a plaque with a prayer for judges by the world's best-known Albanian, Mother Teresa. The iconic nun was born Anjezë Gonxhe Bojaxhiu, about 140 miles away in Skopje, North Macedonia, which at the time of her birth in 1910 was part of the Kosovo division of the Ottoman Empire.

Strikingly, the court holding cell was a cage-like structure situated in the room itself, where the defendant would sit during hearings and trials.

Mother Teresa's "Prayer for Judges" reads in part:

Lord,
listen to my prayer for judges.
They have to listen to so many stories:
give them the ears to hear the honest truth.
They have to judge justly
Like King Solomon:
give them the required wisdom.
They have to condemn cruelty and injustice:
give them compassion and power.
They must take … freedom away
[from] those who have done evil:
give them hope not to desolate those condemned.

Albania has come a long way since the fall of the communist regime. But many of my Albanian colleagues had hoped that after three decades, they might be closer to the just and prosperous society they had envisioned.

Zef, who now is in Washington, DC, working for the US government, never wanted to leave Albania. But he said when he was forced to escape in 1995, it was not "the time for justice in Albania."

At that time, many of his friends wondered why he was "fighting" the president. "Just do what he wants you to do, and you'll have whatever you want for your family," they said.

But he stated that if he had not followed his conscience, he simply could not have lived with himself.

"Thanks to America, thanks to Roger and his friends, I am alive," he said.

"I am blessed that I had such good friends: Roger, Katoo, and Sam Ericsson, John Johnson, Richard Schifter, people at the US Embassy. Very blessed," said Zef.

"I have been so inspired—and surprised—by how much they love Albania."

EPILOGUE

ON MAY 19, 2021, US Secretary of State Antony Blinken announced the "public designation" of Sali Berisha due to "his involvement in significant corruption," banning him from travel to the US under a new anti-corruption law.

Berisha, who is no longer in office, countered with a defamation lawsuit against Blinken. The former president and prime minister contends the sanctions are payback for his opposition to the influence of George Soros' Open Society Foundations on Albania.

The US also publicly designated Berisha's spouse, Liri Berisha, his son, Shkelzen Berisha, and his daughter, Argita Berisha Malltezi.

"In his official capacity as Prime Minister of Albania in particular, Berisha was involved in corrupt acts, such as misappropriation of public funds and interfering with public processes, including using his power for his own benefit and to enrich his political allies and his family members at the expense of the Albanian public's confidence in their government institutions and public officials," wrote the Biden administration secretary of state.

Blinken said Berisha's "own rhetoric demonstrates he is willing to protect himself, his family members, and his political allies at the expense of independent investigations, anticorruption efforts, and accountability measures."

"With this designation, I am reaffirming the need for accountability and transparency in Albania's democratic institutions, government processes, and the actions of Albanian public officials," he said.

Blinken said the designation of Berisha "reaffirms the US commitment to supporting political reforms key to Albania's democratic institutions."

"The United States continues to stand with the people of Albania," he said. "The Department will continue to use authorities like this to promote accountability for corrupt actors in this region and globally."

In Berisha's interview with the New York Post in February 2022,[50] the former Albanian president—who shut down newspapers, removed a chief justice from office for adhering to the rule of law, and was found by the US government to have stolen an election—said he was outraged by the allegations by Blinken.

"Never in my life was I accused by a person or an institution of corruption," Berisha said. "The opposite was true. I worked very closely with the US government in fighting corruption."

ACKNOWLEDGMENTS

THIS HAS BEEN A LIFE'S journey that only God could have orchestrated. My gratitude first goes to him for:

1. Preparing me long in advance through all the molding and shaping experiences he led me through to be ready when the call came.

2. Sending two fax letters from different corners of the globe on the same day and following it up the next day with a video about Albania.

3. Hearing my cries for help and answering all my prayers.

4. Allowing me to have the privilege of seeing his love for the Albanian people through numerous miracles.

Thank you to Art Moore Jr. for sending me that first invitation to Bulgaria and then the fax to come to Albania—and now coming full circle to write this story to share with others. The gratitude both Katoo and I feel toward him for all these life-changing opportunities is fathomless.

Thank you to Sam Ericsson for insisting I go along on the first trip to Bulgaria and for saying yes to becoming the founding president of Advocates International. Sam was a master networker and never shied from calling on heads of state around the world to offer his services. It is because of his undaunted spirit and ability to encourage people that Advocates has Christian lawyers serving on every continent of the world. His Advocates staff in Washington, DC was a great support to the work in Albania.

The effort to help train the judges required a whole community of friends, family, and colleagues. My law partners were so gracious to give me the freedom to work on the judicial conferences and be gone for weeks at a time. My assistant, Linda Wood, tirelessly created and typed all kinds of documents and letters. My partners and staff took Albanian judges on boat trips and hosted them in their homes. Partner Matt Lind accompanied me on one of my trips. A special thanks to partner John Johnson and his family for spending nine months living in Tirana to come alongside judges and lawyers in Albania.

Our church family regularly helped host judges when they came to Poulsbo for weeks of learning about the United States and its judicial system. They made the Albanians feel so welcome, helping prepare meals, driving vans donated by our local Ford dealership, hosting boat excursions and opening their homes. Our pastor, Marc Pearson, accompanied me to Albania, ate lamb brains, and was a natural at fitting in with the Albanian culture. He even opened his back yard to accommodate an impromptu soccer game when he and Carol hosted judges for dinner.

How can I ever give Washington state Chief Justice Bob Utter and Betty enough thanks for all the support, dedication, and selfless sacrifice and energy put into the countless trips to Albania. Because Bob was willing to lend his stature on the spur of the moment to answer many calls for help, Albanian judges have survived many attacks on their independence. Along with Bob and Betty, I want to thank US federal Judge Paul Magnuson and his wife, Elaine, of Minneapolis, and US Court of Appeals Judge John Walker of Connecticut for the numerous trips they have made to Albania. These men give credence to the rule of law in our country. Thank you to all the teams of judges and lawyers who have poured out their hearts to help a fledgling judiciary learn the principles of the rule of law. Every one of them has built meaningful relationships with Albanians and have made our task a joy.

We are very grateful to the Weyerhaeuser Corporation for helping to fund that first judicial conference so long ago. The phone call from the company's Steward Foundation was the lifeline we needed at a crucial time.

Thank you to my sons, Wade and Toby, for your patience and understanding in your teen years. And as adults, Wade, for helping to supply paperweights and plaques as gifts for judges. Also, to both of you, thank you for accompanying me to see for yourself the incredible hospitality of these wonderful people. Over the twenty-five-plus years and more than fifty trips to Albania, many friends and other family members have come to Albania to help. Thank you.

Thank you to the judges of the US Supreme Court, Washington state Supreme Court, Kitsap County Superior Court, and Kitsap County District Court for hosting the Albanian judges and showing them how our legal system operates.

In the beginning, the Washington State Bar Association stepped up to donate enormous amounts of paper, which the Albanian Supreme Court needed to write their opinions. We thank them for acknowledging Roger's life work in Albania by awarding him The Award of Merit in September 2019.

It has been a great privilege to work alongside several of Albania's presidents: Rexhep Meidani, Alfred Moisiu, Bamir Topi, and Bujar Nishani.

And finally, my heartfelt thanks to the many Albanian Supreme

Court and Constitutional Court judges and all the members of the judicial system of the Republic of Albania. The experience of working with each of you, building deep friendships and seeing Albania emerge to become a country accepted into NATO, has been the highlight of my life. Thank you, Chief Justice Zef Brozi, for sacrificing so much for the principles of democracy and the independence of the judiciary. Thanks to Chief Justice Thimio Kondi, who was truly a good man and who did a great deal to further democracy in his country. Thank you to Supreme Court Chief Justices Shpresa Becaj and Xhezair Zaganjori for their friendship and wonderful hospitality every time we were invited to Tirana. Thank you all. I salute you!

NOTE: Because Roger now suffers from Parkinson's Disease and associated dementia, Katoo has written these words of thanks and asks for forgiveness if she has left anything or anyone out.

ENDNOTES

1   Atkinson, Rick. *The Long Gray Line: The American Journey of West Point's Class of 1966* (Houghton Mifflin Company, 1989)

2   "Commander of U.S. troops in Vietnam," Chicago Tribune, July 19, 2005, https://www. chicagotribune.com/news/ct-xpm-2005-07-19-0507190266-story.html.

3   "William C. Westmoreland Is Dead at 91; General Led U.S. Troops in Vietnam," New York Times, July 20, 2005, https://www.nytimes.com/2005/07/20/world/asia/william-c-westmoreland-is-dead-at-91-general-led-us-troops-in.html.

4   Özyurt Ulutaş, Selcen. "The Other Face of the Communist Regime: Concentration Camps in Bulgaria according to CIA Reports 1944-1955." Uluslararası Suçlar ve Tarih Dergisi / International Crimes 20, (2019): 75-93.

5   "300,000 Albanians Pour into Streets to Welcome Baker," *New York Times*, June 12, 1991, https:// www.nytimes.com/1991/06/23/world/300000-albanians-pour-into-streets-to-welcome-baker.html.

6   See Drizari, Nelo, "Scanderbeg; his life, correspondence, orations, victories, and philosophy," (National Press, 1968)

7   Ménage, V.L., "Some Notes on the Devshirme," Bulletin of the School of Oriental and African Studies, University of London, Vol. 29, No. 1 (1966), 64-78

8   See Bill Hamilton, *Albania: Who Cares?* (Grantham, England: Autumn House, 1992), pp. 50-63

9   Fatjona Mejdini, "Albania to Search for Communist Victims' Bodies," *Balkan Insight*, December 4, 2015, https://balkaninsight.com/2015/12/04/albania-reattempts-to-find-6-000-remains-of-communism-12-03-2015/.

10   "Besa: A Code of Honor. Muslim Albanians Who Rescued Jews During the Holocaust," Yadvashem. org, https://www.yadvashem.org/yv/en/exhibitions/besa/index.asp.

11   Kati, Fabian, director, 2014, *The Hidden Documentary*, One Eyed Production.

12   Alex Crevar, "Paranoid Dictator Built Thousands of Military Bunkers—See Them Now," *National Geographic*, October 9, 2017, https://www.nationalgeographic.com/travel/article/photos-forgotten-military-bunkers.

13   See Bill Hamilton, *Albania: Who Cares?* (Grantham, England: Autumn House, 1992), pp. 37-49

14   "Shqipëri: 26 shkurt 1951 regjimi komunist ekzekuton 22 intelektualë shqiptarë," Radiovaticana. org, February 26, 2010, https://archive.ph/20120910030828/http:/www.radiovaticana.org/ALB/ Articolo.asp?c=360125.

15   See Karataş, Ibrahim, "State-Sponsored Atheism: The Case of Albania during the Enver Hoxha Era," Occasional Papers on Religion in Eastern Europe, George Fox University, Vol. 40: Iss. 6, Article 8 (2020), https://digitalcommons.georgefox.edu/ree/vol40/iss6/8.

16   "History of the Party of Labor of Albania," The Institute of Marxist–Leninist Studies at the Central Committee of the Party of Labour of Albania, 1982, http://ciml.250x.com/archive/pla/english/ history_of_the_party_of_labour_of_albania_second_edition_eng.pdf.

17   Valbona Bezati, "How Albania Became the World's First Atheist Country," Balkan Insight, August 28, 2019, https://balkaninsight.com/2019/08/28/how-albania-became-the-worlds-first-atheist-country/.

18   See "Annual Activities Report 1995," International Commission of Jurists, p. 42, http://www.icj.org/wp-content/uploads/2013/06/ICJ-annual-report-1995-eng.pdf.

19   "Berisha's Government Scapegoats Albanian Press," Committee to Protect Journalists, https://cpj. org/reports/1997/05/berisha/.

20   "Minister of Justice Tries to Halt Judges' Conference," *Albanian Daily News*, July 27, 1995.

21   "Declassified Documents Concerning Albania," Memo to President Clinton from Secretary of State Warren Christopher, Clinton Digital Library, September 8, 1995, https://clinton. presidentiallibraries.us/items/show/101228.

22   Charles Stuart Kennedy, "Interview with Richard Schifter," Association for Diplomatic Studies and Training Foreign Affairs Oral History Project, September 8, 2003, https://memory.loc.gov/ service/mss/mfdip/2007/2007sch02/2007sch02.pdf.

23   "Human Rights in Post-Communist Albania," Human Rights Watch/Helsinki, March 1996, https://www.hrw.org/reports/pdfs/a/albania/albania963.pdf.

24   "Albania Country Report on Human Rights Practices for 1997," U.S. Department of State, January 30, 1998, https://1997-2001.state.gov/global/human_rights/1997_hrp_report/albania.html.

25   "Albania: A call for the release of prisoners of conscience," Amnesty International, November 27, 1996, https://www.amnesty.org/en/wp-content/uploads/2021/06/eur110271996en.pdf.

26   US Department of State diplomatic cable from US Embassy Tirana to the secretary of state, March 1995, http://www.modern-albania.com/wp-content/uploads/2015/05/Selami-01.pdf.

27   Julie McCormick, "Theft charges levied against local attorney," *Kitsap Sun*, July 12, 1996, https:// products.kitsapsun.com/archive/1996/07-12/349774_theft_charges_levied_against_lo.html

28   Travis Baker, "POULSBO: Fire razes building," *Kitsap Sun*, July 16, 1998, https://products. kitsapsun.com/archive/1998/07-16/0058_poulsbo__fire_razes_building.html

29   Christopher Jarvis, "The Rise and Fall of Albania's Pyramid Schemes," *Finance & Development*, A quarterly magazine of the IMF, Vol. 37, No. 1 (March 2000), https://www.imf.org/external/pubs/ ft/fandd/2000/03/jarvis.htm.

30   "Albania Country Report on Human Rights Practices for 1997," U.S. Department of State, January 30, 1998, https://1997-2001.state.gov/global/human_rights/1997_hrp_report/albania.html.

31   "Biography of New Albanian Prime Minister Fatos Nano," US State Department cable, August 8, 1997, https://wikileaks.org/plusd/cables/97TIRANA1976_a.html#par9

32   "The Kosovo refugee crisis: An independent evaluation of UNHCR's emergency preparedness and response," United Nations High Commissioner for Refugees Evaluation and Policy Analysis Unit, February 2000, https://www.unhcr.org/3ba0bbeb4.pdf.

33   See Quanrud, John. *A Sacred Task: Qiriazi and the Albanian National Awakening* (Institute for Albanian and Protestant Studies; 2nd edition, 2015)

34   Besar Likmeta, "Albania Ex-PM's Daughter Takes Legal Route to Riches," *Balkan Insight*, August 22, 2014, https://balkaninsight.com/2014/08/22/albania-ex-pm-s-daughter-takes-legal-route-to-riches/.

35   Mark Brunswick, "Obituary: Dorsey & Whitney's Roger Magnuson at 68," *Star Tribune*, December 4, 2013, https://www.startribune.com/obituary-dorsey-whitney-s-roger-magnuson-at-68/234516611/.

36   "Albania littered with symbolism—in the form of bunkers," *CNN*, March 18, 1997, http://www.cnn.com/WORLD/9703/18/albania.bunkers/index.html.

37   C. Dennison Lane, "Once Upon an Army: The Crisis in the Albanian Army, 1995-1996," Conflict Studies Research Centre, September 2002, https://www.files.ethz.ch/isn/38686/2002_Aug.pdf

38   Abrahams, Fred C. *Modern Albania: From Dictatorship to Democracy in Europe* (New York, USA: New York University Press, 2015, p. 285

39   Joubert, Joseph. *Some of the Thoughts of Joseph Joubert (1867)* (Kessinger Publishing, LLC, November 21, 2009)

40   Green, John Richard. *Essays of Joseph Addison* (New York: The Roger De Coverly Club), https://ia600206.us.archive.org/15/items/cu31924013167428/cu31924013167428.pdf.

41   See Tocqueville, Alexis de. *Democracy in America* (New York: G. Dearborn & Co., 1838)

42   George A. Kelly, "The Political Thought of Lamoignon de Malesherbes,"
Political Theory, Vol. 7, No. 4 (November 1979), pp. 485-508, https://www.jstor.org/stable/191163.

43   Bonhoeffer, Dietrich. *Ethics* (Touchstone; 1st Touchstone ed edition, March 20, 2012), p. 105

44   "Albania: Overview of Political Corruption," Transparency International, https://knowledgehub.transparency.org/assets/uploads/helpdesk/Country_profile_Albania_2014.pdf.

45   "Global Corruption Barometer 2013," Transparency International, https://images.transparencycdn.org/images/2013_GlobalCorruptionBarometer_EN_200525_112757.pdf.

46   Jeffrey M. Jones, "Confidence in U.S. Institutions Down; Average at New Low," Gallup, July 5, 2022, https://news.gallup.com/poll/394283/confidence-institutions-down-average-new-low.aspx.

47   "Judicial Watch: State Department Records Show Obama Administration Helped Fund George Soros' Left-Wing Political Activities in Albania," April 4, 2018, https://www.judicialwatch.org/judicial-watch-doj-records-show-obama-administration-helped-fund-george-soros-left-wing-political-activities-albania/.

48   Miranda Devine, "Antony Blinken's horrific stain on Albania and it's all for George Soros," *New York Post*, February 6, 2022, https://nypost.com/2022/02/06/antony-blinkens-horrific-stain-on-albania-and-its-all-for-george-soros/.

49   "Sam Ericsson: Advocate for Today's Testament," *Washington Post*, July 24, 1993, https://www.washingtonpost.com/archive/local/1993/07/24/sam-ericsson-advocate-for-todays-testament/12215c93-2986-4ee8-af1d-0e4fac14b536/.

50   Devine, "Antony Blinken."

July 29, 1969: Departing Italy for Norway in brother Jerry Sherrard's Alpha Romeo Spider.

September 1969: Roger in Vietnam.

Sailing with Washington State Supreme Court justices and US Supreme Court Justice John Paul Stevens (Back row, left to right: Betty Utter, Justice Stevens at the helm, Washington State Supreme Court Justice Robert Utter, Jeff Tolman. Center row: Katoo Sherrard, Roger Sherrard, and others).

Albanian Supreme Court Justice Zef Brozi, right, roasting a lamb on a spit in honor of his new friend Roger Sherrard (Fall 1992).

Zef and Roger on a bunker (1993).

Nico and Lillian Mirdita with Roger.

Albanian farmer.

Roger and attorney Charlie Wiggins picking up the gavels at Chicago O'Hare International Airport (1993).

1993 judicial conference team (Left to right: Judge John Braxton, Roger Sherrard, author Frank Peretti, Texas Supreme Court Justice Raul Gonzalez (behind), North Carolina Judge John McCormick, Charles Wiggins, and Jim Noble of Santa Fe, New Mexico.

Albanian Supreme Court Justice Zef Brozi looking over the first Albanian Judicial Conference manual (1993).

Judicial conference (Left to right: Albanian Supreme Court Justice Thimio Kondi, Philadelphia Judge John Braxton, translator Benny

Interview with Father Zef Pllumi in 1993 (Left to right: Lillian Mirdita, Father Zef Pllumi, and Roger Sherrard).

Tirana courthouse.

Planning meeting before the second Albanian Judicial Conference in 1994 (Right to left: Kyle and Matilda Tromanhauser, Roger Sherrard, Justice Thimio Kond, Chief Justice Zef Brozi, Justice Petrit Plloci, other Albanian judges).

Georgia Court of Appeals Judge Dorothy Beasley with attorney and later Washington State Supreme Court Justice Charlie Wiggins (1994).

Albanian Judicial Conference team in 1994 meets with Albanian President Sali Berisha in his office (Left to right: Jim Noble; Judge John Braxton, Judge Dorothy Beasley, Justice Raul Gonzalez; Justice Robert Utter, Kyle Tromanhauser, Albanian President Sali Berisha, Sam Ericsson, Roger Sherrard, Charles Wiggins, Justice Zef Brozi, presidential staff).

Albanian Judicial Conference 1994 (Front row, left to right: two participants, Katoo Sherrard, Roger Sherrard, Justice Raul Gonzalez. Back row, left to right: Mark Spengler, University of the Nations; Jim Noble; Sam Ericsson; Judge Dorothy Beasley; Charles Wiggins; Judge John Braxton; Justice Petrit Plloci; Kyle Tromanhauser.

Mock trial at 1994 judicial conference.

Sam Ericsson leading a breakout group discussion at the 1994 conference.

Albanian Justice Petrit Plloci receiving his judicial robe from Washington State Justice Robert Utter and Albanian Supreme Court Chief Justice Zef Brozi.

Roger with Zef Brozi and his new wife Diana in Zef's Supreme Court office (1995).

Attorney John Johnson and Roger with Petrit Plloci, celebrating Petrit's victory in Parliament, tabling the removal of the three Supreme Court justices.

Roger and Albanian President Rexhep Meidani going head-to-head to see who is tallest.

Eduart Selami (front right) and wife Peggy with Roger and Katoo, Zef and Diana Brozi on Lake Tahoe as the guests of Roger's cousin, Gary Sherrard.

The 2001 election law team (Left to right: Toby Sherrard, Florida Judge John Kuder; Thimio Kondi's driver "Michael Schumacher," Minnesota attorney Roger Magnuson.

Albanian President Alfred Moisiu (third from left) awards the Special Civil Merits Medal to US District Judge Paul Magnuson, Roger Sherrard, and US Appeals Court Judge John Walker in 2005.

Roger and Katoo at lunch with Albanian President Bujar Nishani (second from left) and Albanian Supreme Court Justice Xhezair Zaganjori in 2016.